"*Strategies from Heaven's Throne* sets the reader on a new journey. Sandie Freed communicates a path that many have longed to walk on but very few have actually found. It is called the path of glory. This book is filled with anointing, revelation and wisdom on how to walk and communicate in a different realm than we normally do. During this season in which we must have the sevenfold Spirit of God working mightily within our lives and our lampstand burning brightly, *Strategies from Heaven's Throne* encourages us to get into a place where the glory dwells and the river of God flows so that we can be a light to the world around us. An excellent book for this hour!"

Chuck D. Pierce, president, Glory of Zion International Ministries, Inc.; watchman, Global Harvest Ministries

"Sandie Freed's newest book serves as a war manual for those who want to walk in 'deliberate' Christianity, waging purposeful warfare. It's for those who want a greater level of the glory of the Lord in and through their lives. It makes a great addition to Sandie's other powerful books, *Destiny Thieves* and *Dream On*."

Steve Shultz, founder, The Elijah List, *Elijah Rain* magazine, *Prophetic.TV*

"*Strategies from Heaven's Throne* is perhaps the most important of the recent books Sandie Freed has written. The keen eye of a prophet is evident as she identifies and dissects the current situational need of the Church and the world, then offers clear and compelling instruction in how to adjust and forge ahead in the days before us.

"In her introduction, Sandie states that 'we cannot fight today's battles with yesterday's victories.' Nonetheless, most of the Church is still attempting that impossible feat. Until and unless we are willing to let go of the past and press into God for battle strategies that are greater than the plans of the enemy, we cannot prevail.

"The revelation and information provided in this book will help every believer recognize mind-set patterns or hindrances that keep us from responding to what the Spirit is saying to the Church. My prayer is that *Strategies from Heaven's Throne* will be widely read and faithfully applied so that the Church of God is prepared to fight and win the victories ordained for her."

Dr. Jim Davis, president,
Christian International Apostolic Network

Strategies from
HEAVEN'S THRONE

Claiming the Life God Wants for You

SANDIE FREED

Chosen
Grand Rapids, Michigan

Published by Chosen Books
A division of Baker Publishing Group
P.O. Box 6287, Grand Rapids, MI 49516-6287
www.chosenbooks.com

Printed in the United States of America

Library of Congress Cataloging-in-Publication Data
Freed, Sandie, 1951–
      Strategies from heaven's throne : claiming the life God wants for you / Sandie Freed.
          p.   cm.
      Includes bibliographical references.
      ISBN 10: 0-8007-9430-3 (pbk.)
      ISBN 978-0-8007-9430-9 (pbk.)
      1. Christian life. I. Title.
BV4501.3.F737 2007
248.4—dc22   2006037010

Unless otherwise indicated, Scripture is taken from the HOLY BIBLE, NEW INTERNATIONAL VERSION®. NIV®. Copyright © 1973, 1978, 1984 by International Bible Society. Used by permission of Zondervan. All rights reserved.

Scripture marked NKJV is taken from the New King James Version. Copyright © 1982 by Thomas Nelson, Inc. Used by permission. All rights reserved.

Scripture marked NLT is taken from the *Holy Bible*, New Living Translation, copyright © 1996. Used by permission of Tyndale House Publishers, Inc., Wheaton, Illinois 60189. All rights reserved.

Scripture marked KJV is taken from the King James Version of the Bible.

CONTENTS

FOREWORD

Sandie has made a tremendous contribution to the Body of Christ. In this book, you will learn how to discover the hindrances that keep you from possessing your full inheritance in Christ Jesus. The truths and principles presented will empower you to leave your wilderness, cross over your Jordan and enter into your Promised Land of blessing and prophetic fulfillment.

I have been fully knowledgeable of Sandie's life, family and ministry for nearly twenty years. I can assure you that the truths presented here were not just gleaned from reading a book. They are truths that have been proven by living and practicing them in her daily life and ministry.

Sandie keeps the flow of her book interesting by presenting many visions and personal experiences. As you read, you will gain insight concerning how to fulfill the scriptural command to go from glory to glory until you are conformed to the image of Christ and fulfill your ministry destiny.

This book will give you great enlightenment and encouragement, as it will to Christians around the world. As children of God, we are made joint-heirs with Christ Jesus, who promised those who overcome all things the right to sit down with Him on His Father's throne. This means that we have throne room rights and authority. To appropriate and exercise these throne room rights, we need *Strategies from Heaven's Throne.*

God bless you, Sandie, for taking the time and effort to put these truths into a book. Because of it, many Christians will be blessed and move forward in their journey of fulfilling their calling and ministry in Christ Jesus.

Dr. Bill Hamon
Founder of Christian International Ministries and
author of *Day of the Saints* and eight other major books

ACKNOWLEDGMENTS

As always, I wish to thank my husband, Mickey, who continues to love and support me in whatever I do. Like my father, who today is with Jesus in heaven, Mickey never allows me to settle for less than I can be. I thank my mother, Dena Davis, who continues to be the most courageous woman of wisdom and insight that I know, and my sister, Pam Garris, for her continued support and loyalty. I am thankful to my kids, Kim and Matt Putman, for their ongoing support in so many ways, and to our covenant partners of Zion Ministries, who make it easy for me to remain productive for the Lord. I want to give very special thanks to my personal intercessors—Paula Bledsoe, Vicki Caldwell, Shelley Posner, Kathy Shaw, Sarah Amanor, Natalie Byers and Norma Guitierrez—who cover me daily in prayer as I make these endeavors to put my thoughts into print. I am always thankful for my spiritual parents, Bishop and Mom Evelyn Hamon, for continuing to push me out of my comfort zones, and for Dr. Jim and Jeanie Davis, who remain an oversight of accountability and also our precious friends. I am especially grateful for my Chosen Books editor and friend, Jane Campbell, for her ongoing encouragement and belief in this book. Also, I am very thankful for Grace Sarber for the many hours she spent in the preliminary editing process, and Christy Phillippe for supporting and directing me through the finalization of this project.

INTRODUCTION

Of all the twelve tribes of Israel, one tribe was ordained and destined to understand the times and seasons—the tribe of Issachar. Issachar was the ninth son of Jacob and the fifth by his wife Leah. One translation of his name is "one to be rewarded."[1] The Scripture describes the sons of Issachar as those who "understood the times and knew what Israel should do" (1 Chronicles 12:32).

Today we believers are being rewarded with an Issachar anointing. As sons of Issachar, we have the very same ability to understand the times in which we live and to know what to do!

But while many of us understand the times, we need more revelation on what to do with what we understand about those times. In other words, we need fresh strategies in this season to ensure that we properly respond to the direction given from the Lord.

What do I mean by strategies? A *strategy* is "a plan or method of achieving a specific goal." *Webster's* also defines it as "the use of a stratagem" and "the art of planning and directing large-scale military movement and operation."[2]

Most Christians understand that we are God's army. We are aware that we have an enemy, Satan. We understand our spiritual authority and, therefore, exercise dominion over the powers of darkness. Being seated with Christ in heavenly places gives us a "throne" of authority (see Ephesians 2:6). We need, however, to remain continually before *His* throne in order to receive fresh strategies for the battles we face today.

We cannot fight today's battles with yesterday's victories. Each day is a new challenge, and we need fresh strategies from the throne, a meal of daily manna, to empower us for the battles that lie ahead.

Strategy is also defined as "having a *stratagem*," which is "a scheme or trick for surprising or deceiving an enemy."[3] Dear ones, the enemy has deceived us long enough. It is time to gain strategies to deceive him and thwart his plans. Heavenly strategies help us outthink and outsmart the devil!

Isaiah Gained Strategy in the Throne Room

The prophet Isaiah received strategies from heaven's throne. In Isaiah 6, the prophet describes how he found himself before God's throne. He describes the throne room, and through Isaiah's account, we learn several things about approaching the throne.

First, King Uzziah had to die before the prophet could fully witness God's glory. Isaiah experienced the death of "an old thing" and in that same season was finally able to see the "Lord seated on a throne, high and exalted" (Isaiah 6:1). Wow! Imagine that!

What has to die in us before we are able to embrace a throne room experience, to gain further understanding of His glory and receive our calling? Dear ones, many times we have to let the old thing die so we can receive His life. Only then are we really able to see God high and lifted up—above our situations and circumstances.

Isaiah shifted into a new place full of God's glory. He witnessed the throne room life. Now, who would ever desire to leave a place like that? Wouldn't you just like to bring your sleeping bag and camp there a while? Imagine observing the angels crying out, "Holy, holy, holy is the Lord of Hosts." Witnessing this glory and the doorposts moving at His voice would cause us, like Isaiah, to be totally awestruck.

But, oh my goodness, what about that angel with tongs and the hot coal? He touched it to Isaiah's lips—how painful that must have been! The angel declared, "See, this coal has touched your lips. Now your guilt is removed, and your sins are forgiven" (Isaiah 6:7, NLT). Isaiah had to be cleansed from impure thoughts, sins and iniquity before he could approach the throne and be given strategies to proceed into his destiny.

After he was cleansed, he heard the voice of the Lord saying, "Whom shall I send? And who will go for us?" And Isaiah said, "Here am I. Send me!" (Isaiah 6:8). And the Lord sent him, complete with fresh strategies to move mountains and change governments. So Isaiah's requirement as one who was "sent" was to first move past the death of an old thing, to visit the Lord in His throne room, to witness His glory and to be cleansed from impure thoughts, sins and iniquity. Isaiah desired to be sent forth, but his sending only came because the other steps had been accomplished first.

Are we willing to endure this harsh and painful cleansing? Or will we shut our mouths, roll up our sleeping gear and run for dear life? Do we have a choice? I think not. We must realize that in order to be "sent," we first will have to be cleansed.

Isaiah was sent out with God's authority from the throne room. This prophet had a fresh strategy, fresh empowerment and fresh direction after his throne room experience. Isaiah was "sent" from the throne room to reform political and social wrongs, to confront witches and soothsayers, to denounce the wealthy and ungodly and to denounce ungodly kings. He also foretold of the Messiah and gave specific prophetic instruction to the godly kings. Wow! Now that is what I call heavenly strategies!

We are living in an apostolic age. The word *apostle* means "sent one." Like Isaiah, our authority in the spirit realm is given to us because we are sent out with authority. There are some differences, however. The strategies Isaiah received were somewhat different from warfare strategies we might receive from the Lord today. Isaiah gave prophetic demonstrations, such as going barefoot for three years and wearing only a loincloth (see Isaiah 20:2–6). He was instructed to do this during a time in biblical history when society measured status by meticulous dress codes.

Today status is measured in similar ways, but a prophet who wore only a loincloth would most likely be put in jail for indecent exposure! We must hear God's instruction for our time today, not times past, and in order to hear Him clearly, we, like Isaiah, must be positioned at His throne.

A New Door Has Opened

The throne room awaits us. The door that opens to this place where we will find new strategies and new understanding awaits our entrance.

Are you ready to receive fresh strategy for your life? Are you ready to gain new direction from the throne of God? The Lord is inviting us to come up to a new level because He wants to show us some new things. His voice is as a trumpet sounding forth, calling us up into a new dimension, before His throne.

After this I looked, and there before me was a door standing open in heaven. And the voice I had first heard speaking to me like a trumpet said, *"Come up here*, and I will show you what must take place after this."* At once I was in the Spirit, and there before me was *a throne in heaven* with *someone sitting on it.*

Revelation 4:1–2, emphasis mine

1

THE HIGHWAY OF HOLINESS

A highway shall be there, and a road, and it shall be called the Highway of Holiness.

Isaiah 35:8, NKJV

It was time for Sunday morning worship. My normal pre-service routine involved double-checking on our worship team. I slowly and quietly pried open the door into the sanctuary, certain that our team was ready to begin the worship service. As I observed them gathering at the altar, I smiled and silently prayed, *Thank You, Lord, for their faithfulness. I ask You to bless this service with Your divine presence and empower each member of the worship team to be a carrier of Your power and anointing.*

Each team member seemed to explode with excited smiles as they approached their designated instruments and positions. Our worship leader checked his keyboard and the other necessary sound equipment. With a final nod to the soundman, his fingers made their way to the keys that would open up the heavenlies with corporate worship. As expected, the keyboard resonated with the most incredible tones. The air vibrated with God's glory!

I returned to my office to pray with my husband, and together we sought the Lord for His last-minute instructions. The music began. The service was beginning. It was time to meet the Lord as we worshiped.

We entered the sanctuary. As I made my way to the front row, God's presence was so strong that it swept me off my feet. I found myself landing prostrate in front of the altar. I was totally captivated by the presence of the Holy Spirit; obviously He had something to reveal to me.

Unaware of my natural surroundings, I was totally caught away in a heavenly vision. I still search for the adequate words to paint a picture of the majestic vision I saw. Before my eyes, a chariot of fire swept down from the heavens. It was the most glorious sight! The flames appeared to leap from the chariot, lighting up the heavenlies so that a golden glow encircled the chariot. Each flame seemed to carry within itself a remarkable ability to release light into the atmosphere. As the flames leapt, in their places other "fresh" flames would ignite upon the chariot, and new flames also descended from heaven upon the chariot to ignite where previous flames had been. The glorious glow from the flames lit a highway in the skies where the chariot traveled. The chariot was constantly lit with a fresh fire, a fire that never burned out. It was an eternal burning vehicle of glory, burning with a fire that would not be quenched.

The chariot also sparkled with a richness of gold that is almost indescribable. The "depth" of the golden color somehow symbolized a most profound depth of God's glory, so deep that His glory extended into eternity with no boundaries. Similar to the weightiness of solid gold, the chariot was draped with the heaviness, the stability and the majesty of His divine glory.

The chariot swept through the skies as if it were circling the globe. It seemed to be searching for a landing strip. The vehicle of golden fire circled and then re-circled repeatedly, finally heading toward the earth as if to land. But not landing, the fiery presence hurled back into the heavenlies and circled once more. Finally, the chariot of glory made a direct descent and attempted to make its landing. As it reached the earth, I noticed that it did not actually plant firmly on the ground but, rather, hovered a few inches above the ground. Now the chariot was directly in front of me, and I could examine its characteristics more closely.

The chariot seemed to have a personality all its own. It appeared to be alive and active with a strong determination to move forward and accomplish its mission on the earth. Two eyes appeared in front of the chariot like two headlights on modern-day vehicles. The eyes were focused on the ground, looking at a road that was inappropriate for landing or traveling. The road was full of potholes and rocks. It had so many gaping gulches and deep crevices that absolutely no vehicle could travel on it. Because the road was not properly prepared for travel, the chariot seemed saddened. I sensed that the chariot desired to go forth, and yet it grieved because there was no highway on which it could travel.

Suddenly I knew the purpose of this vision. God was seeking a highway upon which to release His glory! I felt the compassion of the Father who desired to show His glory to His precious children, but no path had been prepared. I was overwhelmed with a sense of urgency, and I knew that He wanted to come now. I also was aware that the road needed proper preparation so that His glory could travel upon it. As I continued to observe the vision, I began to cry out within myself, *Lord, how do we prepare the way? Help me to understand how to prepare You a place!*

I then saw miles of men and women all dressed in solid white garments and standing in rows on each side of the road. God revealed to me that these were the apostles and prophets of the Most High God. On one side of the road were the prophets, and on the opposite side were the apostles. I was amazed at the number of white robes lining the road, which extended like an endless highway into mountains and plains.

A sound from the chariot caught my attention. It was the sound of a fresh burst of flames being ignited. The chariot was becoming "fired up" to move forward down this road. I thought to myself, *How are we going to fix this road for God's glory to travel upon it?*

Suddenly the apostles and prophets began to lie down in the road. One by one, they flung their bodies on top of the unleveled road to fill every gulch and crevice with their bodies. They did not hesitate to hurl themselves on top of sharp rocks and briars, to lay down their lives as a Highway of Holiness for the chariot of God's glory. My thoughts and emotions leaped inside myself. *What bravery! What commitment! I only wish that I were that determined.*

I was overwhelmed with a sense of destiny and spiritual fortitude. I found myself involved in the sacrifice, this death-to-self experience. I quickly threw my own body down before the chariot, not caring how much pain or suffering I endured. I only knew that I wanted His glory and would gladly lay down my life for it.

At that moment of tremendous sacrifice, a level highway stretched out for the chariot to travel upon. The chariot landed on the road and sped forth. Ignited with a fresh thrust of fire, the chariot blazed a trail upon the new foundation of the apostles and prophets who were willing to lay down their lives for His glory.

I abruptly became aware of my natural surroundings. My thoughts ran amok. *O God, does this vision mean that You are requiring more from me? How can I possibly do more? Haven't I laid down my life already for You? I feel as if I have already died a thousand times.* (Okay, I knew I was about to shift into a martyr syndrome, so I caught myself from moving into self-pity.)

In response to my plea for understanding the vision, God spoke to me over a period of time:

> My desire is to move you into a greater level of My glory. The new anointing that I have for all My people will require each of them to embrace My "new thing." It is a costly anointing, and it will require a price to be paid to achieve the greater glory. I am going to give My children many different throne room strategies that will reveal ways to defeat their enemies and experience greater levels of My glory. They will lay down their lives and be the foundation upon which I will build. I will also show My people a new structure of building, and they will have a heart to build as in the days of Nehemiah. Because they will pay the price to change and remove themselves from an old method of building, I will release to them a new mantle of authority. This mantle will empower them with a new leadership. They will become a people who embrace heaven's divine government. As they implement My government upon the earth, they will shift and align with My heavenly purposes. The new mantle will restructure their lives, their ministries, their culture, their businesses and their families. As I move My people from glory to glory, they will be changed more and more into My image.

Since the day of the vision, the Lord has been drawing me closer to Him. I have developed a fresh hunger for revelation that has empowered me to shift into His full plan for my life.

The Glory of the Lord

While I have sought His glory, at the same time I have not fully understood what God's glory really represents. The word *glory* in Scripture has several different meanings. The expression of *glory* to which I refer in this book is the glory that is revealed when heaven touches earth, or as Bob Sorge says, "the invasion of God's reality into the human sphere."[1] This is when God takes His glory, which exists in heaven in divine time, pushes it through the natural atmosphere and natural time (our time on earth) and establishes the supernatural. In other words, God takes what already exists in heaven—the spoken Word, which is already in existence, alive and active—and pushes it through the natural realm to manifest the promise we have awaited. I call this one of God's "suddenlies," when God releases His glory at the appointed time and "suddenly" reveals the magnificence of who He is and what He does.

A practical example is in the realm of healing. As God invades the earth with His glory, He releases what He has already written and decreed concerning healing. Then as we mix our faith with His Word, He causes the Word to press through the natural realm to release a supernatural miracle. Hallelujah!

The Lord has already declared that all flesh shall see His glory. He is simply waiting for those who will pay the price and lay down their agendas, embrace present truth and receive His glory.

> "And the glory of the LORD will be revealed, and all mankind together will see it. For the mouth of the LORD has spoken."
>
> Isaiah 40:5

> "For the earth will be filled with the knowledge of the glory of the LORD, as the waters cover the sea."
>
> Habakkuk 2:14

Get ready, saints! The heavens are about to invade the earth, and the whole earth will be filled with the knowledge of the glory of the Lord!

The Kingdom Quest

Alive, active and full of power, the chariot in my vision represented God's vehicle of glory to be released upon the earth. Much like the written Word of God being alive with a "living power," the chariot had an active part in fulfilling God's purposes on the earth.

> The chariots of God are twenty thousand, even thousands of angels: the Lord is among them, as in Sinai, in the holy place. Thou hast ascended on high, thou hast led captivity captive: thou hast received gifts for men; yea, for the rebellious also, that the LORD God might dwell among them.
>
> Psalm 68:17–18, KJV

This passage in Psalms states that when God's chariots appear, thousands of angels will come with Him. It also tells us that as He invades the earth with His glory, He leads captivity captive. In other words, at the same time God reveals His glory, thousands of angels are released to become ministering spirits to the saints upon the earth who colabor with His plans and purposes. As a result of His glory, we are loosed from bondage, prison cell doors are opened and the oppressed are set free!

The vision of the chariot and His glory affected my life in such a dynamic way that I have been on a "Kingdom quest" ever since. I knew from the vision that I would be a part of ushering in His presence and glory in a new way; in fact, I would be a pioneer to help prepare the way. The process would involve a death-to-the-flesh experience. I was going to be required to press beyond my natural understanding, to renew my mind and to shift into a Kingdom mentality. It was time to rise up to another level of spiritual maturity and authority and move past my old patterns of behavior. Since God revealed to me that vision, I have been seeking the King and His Kingdom with a fresh passion, more determined than ever to press into a more intimate relationship with Him.

God's Bravehearts

Do you remember the movie *Braveheart* with the actor Mel Gibson? It tells the story of a man, William Wallace, who fought bravely for what he believed amidst the extreme injustice that England forced upon his beloved Scotland.

As a child, Wallace had been socially educated in "tradition." Tradition dictates our future, but only if we allow it. Wallace fought against the injustice and discrimination of the times, which were the results of "tradition." He challenged his present-day hierarchy of injustice, the paradigms of society and religious beliefs.

Wallace ultimately laid down his life for a higher cause. His capture and death were tragic. He was labeled as a traitor, but in his heart he had not betrayed what he knew was noble and just. He was a pioneer in freedom and new ways of thinking, and he was a hallmark of bravery. Wallace followed his heart and his passion—and a Braveheart was birthed.

The vision of the chariot that God gave me was not just for me alone. It was for all those who are called to become God's Bravehearts. These are God's chosen ones—*all* of us believers—who will press through fears and hindrances and fight spiritually for a cause. Like William Wallace, we might even be required to lay down our lives for something greater than we have seen before.

Wilderness Voices Preparing the Way

God is very committed to change, especially when it is we who need changing! He is invading the earth with His glory, and this invasion requires each of us to change by being prepared and matured to a new level.

But we do not desire change. As long as our lives are fine, our children are prospering, our needs are met and we are experiencing great blessing, why change? Who in their right mind wants to move from that place of comfort and success? We may believe that we are ready to ascend to higher levels and experience the fullness of God's glory, but most of us are not fully prepared for the changes involved in getting there.

But when we go through a wilderness experience, we become ready to embrace something new. It is usually a wilderness experience that makes us ready to change and prepares our hearts for something greater.

Two thousand years ago, heaven came to earth. Jesus left His Kingdom in heaven to be the Way. Prior to His coming, two prophets came out of the wilderness to prepare the way for the coming of His glory. The prophet Isaiah first sought to prepare the way with his prophetic message, and then John the Baptist picked up where Isaiah left off. The prophets passed the baton in the spiritual race to receive God's fullness; yet most of the people who heard the Good News were too bound in religious tradition to receive the new wine and were, therefore, unprepared for change.

Let's read the truths that Isaiah declared and compare them with the words of John the Baptist:

Isaiah's Declaration:

A voice of one calling: "In the desert prepare the way for the LORD; make straight in the wilderness a highway for our God. Every valley shall be raised up, every mountain and hill made low; the rough ground shall become level, the rugged places a plain. And the glory of the LORD will be revealed, and all mankind together will see it. For the mouth of the LORD has spoken."

Isaiah 40:3–5

John the Baptist's Declaration:

In those days John the Baptist came, preaching in the Desert of Judea and saying, "Repent, for the kingdom of heaven is near." This is he who was spoken of through the prophet Isaiah: "A voice of one calling in the desert, 'Prepare the way for the Lord, make straight paths for him.'"

Matthew 3:1–3

Both prophets were ministering words that indicated change. Both were crying out from wilderness places. And both declared that a way needed to be prepared for God's glory. Notice that Isaiah specifically mentions making a "highway for our God."

We can learn a great deal about preparing the way for God's glory by studying these two Scripture passages:

1. God first builds a highway in our hearts.
2. He then fills in the valleys of our hearts.
3. He examines our hearts and brings down every high place—every area in which the desires of our hearts are above serving Him and achieving His desires.
4. He makes every crooked path straight.
5. He causes every rough place to be made smooth.
6. Then we lay down our lives for Him, for we must decrease so that He might increase.

Our mandate in this season is to receive the clarion call to be those who prepare the way! Let's pick up the baton, receiving the prophetic challenge to be ones who not only are prepared, but who also prepare a way for others to receive God's glory.

Just as John the Baptist faced religious opposition, we also will be persecuted. He confronted a religious structure, a belief system and man's tradition. He boldly preached a "straight-path" message, which involved traveling a highway of holiness. He was a voice that the Lord used to prepare the way for a greater dimension of God's glory on the earth.

Will you also be a voice?

Straight Paths and Smooth Edges

The Hebrew word for "make straight" in the previous Isaiah passage means "to be straight, right, upright, pleasing, good."[2] Another passage, Proverbs 3:5–6, tells us that it is God Himself who straightens out our paths as we trust in Him: "Trust in the LORD with all your heart and lean not on your own understanding; in all your ways acknowledge him, and he will make your paths straight." When we trust Him totally and embrace His direction for our lives—and that means leaving the past behind and following Him—He is committed to "straightening" us out.

God desires to fill in every valley. Each low place in our hearts will be filled to overflowing measures by His love and His Spirit. Every deep crevice of pain, shameful memories and devastation will be full of His glory as He heals us from the past. Every deep canyon in our lives will become a positive confession of "I can do all things through Christ who strengthens me!" and "What the enemy has meant for harm, God has turned around for my good!"

When God says that every mountain will be brought low, He is referring to every high thing in our lives that He has set His face against, such as pride, competition, self-promotion, our own will, our private agendas, our personal ambitions and so on. In other words, He is committed to bringing these things down!

Making the rough places smooth refers to our "rough edges." Do you have any of these? My goodness, I sure do! Most of us are keen at noticing the rough edges of others, but dear ones, it is time to examine our own rough places. When things get "rough," then we can really tell if we have any "rough edges"! Tough times expose tough hearts.

Is there any area in your heart that has become hardened toward the plans of God? Do you feel you have stepped out in faith only to fail? Don't despair! His highway of holiness is a highway of restoration. God has been preparing us for the fullness of His glory. As we are prepared to receive His glory, we in turn prepare others. If you are ready to shift out of this old place of despair, then allow Him to prepare you for the new place that He has provided for you.

Satan Desires to Twist the Straight Paths

Let me add a warning here: The enemy desires to twist every straight way of the Lord. Satan wants to hinder the free flow of God's Spirit and glory. He twists the truth, blinds our eyes so we are unable to see the truth and plugs up our ears so we cannot hear it.

He also persecutes the saints with religious opposition and false accusations. The "religious spirit" attempts to hinder the glorious release of signs, wonders and miracles. This spirit twists the truth concerning present-day revelation and the different ministries of the Holy Spirit. The "religious spirit" causes many of God's people to cling to old doctrine, remain in religious comfort zones and reject all present truth concerning God's divine movement upon the earth.

Don't be deceived by the religious spirit, but rather be determined to be open-minded to the present revelation of truth. We cannot assume that we know everything about God or even how He desires to move. He is doing a "new thing"! (For more information on the "religious spirit," read my book *Destiny Thieves: Defeat Seducing Spirits and Achieve Your Purpose in God*, which is available through Chosen Books.)

God is requiring each of us to rise to a higher level. Many spiritual pioneers are actively pursuing God's presence and glory. They are not allowing the religious spirit to bind them in old wineskins. Tossing tradition to the side, they are moving beyond the theology of man's paradigms and mind-sets while seeking the fullness of His Spirit.

Will you also become one of them? Will you become one of God's Bravehearts who will lay down personal ambition, the fear of failure and the fear of being different and step into the unknown?

Celebrate the Changes

God has been reordering and restructuring my life for as long as I can remember. And yet, all along He has remained faithful to lead me on paths that release increase and enlargement.

I have learned to celebrate the changes God has required in my life. At times, even though I know better, I still fight hard to hold onto what is traditional and comfortable. But He is faithful to confront me with a new way—a living way—and His truth concerning my future. Each change has been coupled with a greater dependence on His Holy Spirit, and yet I am stronger with each transition. I love what Dr. Wanda Turner said in her book *Celebrate Change*: "Mountains pack their bags when they see me coming!"[3]

As an added blessing, He has remained committed to conform me into His image. After all, isn't that what this life is all about—being changed into His image, making a difference and experiencing Him? Certainly there is more, such as fulfilling destiny, possessing the promise and entering into fulfillment, and we will discuss those very things. But all that we desire for complete fulfillment comes only if we are on the correct highway!

There is a High Way, a higher highway that leads to a greater level of His glory. In order for us to bravely advance into our future and see His glory, we must remain on His highway of holiness.

This involves doing business His way, holding church services His way and seeking Him in His way. God is true to His plan, and He does have a way in which He demands things to be done. Those of us who attempt to do Kingdom business the same as usual soon will discover that God has decided to get a new partner. He refuses to act without man, but He works alongside man only as long as He chooses in order to bring about His divine plan.

Let me invite you to make a decision to change and to walk this highway with me. Yes, there will be seasons when we advance into unknown territory. But even though we are required to lay down our lives for Him, He repays the sacrifice with expansion and enlargement. He desires to visit and commune with us while guiding us into truth.

The Great Exchange

A prophetic passage from the book of Isaiah tells us that God desires to perform a great exchange with us:

> The Spirit of the Sovereign LORD is on me, because the LORD has anointed me to preach good news to the poor. He has

sent me to bind up the brokenhearted, to proclaim freedom
for the captives and release from darkness for the prisoners, to proclaim the year of the LORD's favor and the day
of vengeance of our God, to comfort all who mourn, and
provide for those who grieve in Zion—to bestow on them
a crown of beauty instead of ashes, the oil of gladness instead of mourning, and a garment of praise instead of a
spirit of despair.

Isaiah 61:1–3

The Lord is going to give you beauty for your ashes!
He is going to heal every area of your broken heart, empower you with the goodness of the Gospel and release
you from whatever has held you captive. This means that
though you may have been through the fires of affliction
and feel like you are a "crispy critter," He is giving you
beauty!

Remember Job? He was persecuted and abandoned. But
God was faithful to Job. God allowed Job to suffer the fire
of affliction and the ashes, but then the Word states that
all was restored back to Job in greater measure (see Job
42:12–16).

God is going to bless us with increase and expansion.
Now that is a breakthrough strategy straight from God's
throne!

The Highway of Holiness Is a Road of Abundance

Isaiah 35 describes this highway that the Lord has
prepared:

The wilderness and the solitary place shall be *glad* for
them; and the desert shall *rejoice*, and *blossom* as the rose.
It shall blossom *abundantly*, and *rejoice* even with *joy and
singing*: the glory of Lebanon shall be given unto it, the
excellency of Carmel and Sharon, they shall see the *glory*

of the LORD, and the *excellency of our God. Strengthen ye the weak* hands, and *confirm the feeble knees.* Say to them that are of a fearful heart, *Be strong, fear not*: behold, your God will come with vengeance, even God with a recompence; he will come and *save you.* Then the *eyes of the blind shall be opened,* and the *ears of the deaf shall be unstopped.* Then shall *the lame man leap as an hart,* and *the tongue of the dumb sing*: for in *the wilderness shall waters break out, and streams in the desert.* And the *parched ground shall become a pool,* and *the thirsty land springs of water*: in the habitation of dragons, where each lay, shall be grass with reeds and rushes. And an highway shall be there, and a way, and it shall be called *The way of holiness*; the unclean shall not pass over it; but it shall be for those: the wayfaring men, though fools, shall not err therein. No lion shall be there, nor any ravenous beast shall go up thereon, it shall not be found there; but *the redeemed shall walk there: And the ransomed of the* LORD *shall return, and come to Zion with songs and **everlasting joy** upon their heads: they shall obtain joy and gladness, and sorrow and sighing shall flee away.*

Isaiah 35, KJV, emphasis mine

All too often, we prematurely evaluate the roads that God has us travel as difficult, hard and almost impossible to cross. But the Good News is just the opposite! The highway of holiness is a road of abundance, excellence and healing. We need not be fearful-hearted (the opposite of brave-hearted). We can be strong and courageous because God will protect us with a vengeance. As we travel on God's highway, we will have open eyes and ears to see and hear Him by the Spirit, and we will go forth with joy and singing. Hallelujah!

Read Isaiah 35 again and envision yourself traveling God's highway with a brave heart. Take some time to meditate on all the positives along the highway of holiness. Then read it again and boldly declare all that God has prepared for you as you travel His highway.

Pray with Positive Confessions for the Future

At this point, we need to take some time to stop and pray. It is very important to make positive confessions concerning the future. As you pray this prayer, which is based on Isaiah 35, you will negate any negative words spoken about your future. This prayer will drive out fear and empower you with courage and bravery to face your future and receive God's abundant blessings:

> *Lord, as I travel Your highway of holiness, I am confident that You have prepared a highway of life! Although at times I may feel lonely and weak, You have promised to strengthen my feeble knees. If I am fearful, then You encourage me by stating that I need not fear. I am empowered to become strong because You will come with a mighty vengeance and save me from my enemies. Even when I know I am experiencing a wilderness season, the roses will continue to bloom, and You will place joy in my heart because You love me with an everlasting love. I am confident that this way of holiness will become lasting springs of water as You purify my thoughts, deeds and actions. As You sanctify my motives and circumcise my heart anew, You will provide pools of refreshing and draw me ever closer to Yourself. You have promised to protect me from the lion that seeks to destroy me and fools who attempt to deceive me as I travel this pathway of holiness. I will come to Zion, the City of God, with songs of joy and gladness, and all sorrow and sighing will flee away. I pray this prayer in Jesus' name, Amen.*

Come with me on this journey as we travel His higher way, the highway of holiness. This pathway will require time spent before His throne in prayer and supplication. But along this highway, we will find divine strategies for fulfillment.

2

"HELP ME, LORD! I CAN'T SEE WHERE I'M GOING!"

The Spirit of the Sovereign LORD is on me, because the LORD has anointed me to preach good news to the poor. . . . They will be called oaks of righteousness, a planting of the LORD for the display of his splendor.

Isaiah 61:1, 3

Have you ever told God that you needed to see where you were going? Leaving the past behind requires entering into unknown territory, and walking into unknown territory is difficult at best. But leaving familiar surroundings and comfort zones is necessary when God requires the embracing of a new thing or a fresh direction.

I am a person of certainty. I thrive on being sure, steadfast and steady. I also have a need to know. In other words, when I am sure and I know the details concerning a task or project, I am empowered to move forward. When I do not know in advance what is expected of me, however, I fret and worry unnecessarily. I can easily become stuck, and therefore unfruitful, when I am unsure of the situation.

When we are following God, walking in faith and trusting Him in all situations, most of the time we are unsure and do not know the outcome or full direction of His plan. The faith walk is the process of traveling on an unknown and challenging road. That is why it is a walk of faith! Although it is a difficult road to travel, it is a necessary road that builds godly character and greater faith. Walking into unknown territory is part of the process of developing our faith as well as experiencing supernatural breakthroughs.

Abraham: The One Who Crossed Over

Abraham understood what it meant to walk into unknown territory. He left his birthplace and all that was familiar to heed God's call to cross over into a promised land. I have wondered how Abraham remained steadfast, because he did not have a clue where he was headed.

Abraham's walk of faith incorporated leaving his homeland and later actually leaving his father's house. Can you imagine all the emotions involved in this process? Abraham was human, and I am sure that it was very emotional for him as he walked out his destiny. Getting to the other side of emotions—crossing over—can be so challenging that we often choose not to let go of the past. Pressing beyond our emotions is a "crossover" point for all of us during our faith walk. Abraham had developed the ability to see beyond what he was experiencing in the natural. He did not focus on what he saw before him, but rather on what he knew God had told him in the supernatural. This is an attribute we all must have as we follow the Lord into the unknown. Like Abraham, we must depend upon the sensing of the supernatural and not be motivated by what we "feel" or "see" in the natural.

On top of all of that, Abraham had to work through family issues with his nephew, Lot. You may be familiar with the biblical account of Lot and how he chose to live in Sodom, one of the "twin cities of sin." Emotions wreak havoc when a family member chooses to live in sin; and yet Abraham knew that he had to keep moving forward in order to fulfill his divine destiny. When Lot was captured by the four kings, Abraham came to the rescue to deliver Lot's family from slavery. It was at this time in Abraham's life that he was referred to as the "Hebrew," or "one who crosses over" (Genesis 14:13).

It is important to understand why Abraham needed to "cross over" and put on a warfare mantle for his family. First of all, there is the significance of covenant relationship. Natural, blood-related families, as well as the family of God, are covenant-related. Abraham understood the significance of covenant and, therefore, went to war on his nephew's behalf.

It is the same with the Church. We in the Body of Christ are blood-related because of the blood of Jesus. We are, therefore, in covenant with the Lord and with each other. We must understand how important our covenant relationship is with the Lord and never treat it lightly. The Lord will war on our behalf! He has promised to go to battle for us, going ahead of us to defeat our enemies. Our part in keeping covenant with God is to continue to "cross over" into every new place that the Lord instructs us to go. This is how we move forward from glory to glory. We will never stop crossing over; it is a progression of breakthroughs as we embrace one level, or revelation, and move on to the next revelation.

Because Abraham was the father of many nations and our spiritual father, I believe that what he possessed and experienced during his walk of faith and obedience affects our inheritance and destiny today. Spiritually we are Abraham's family (he is the father of our faith), and when he went to battle for the destiny of Lot, he also warred over our destiny. In other words, when he warred against the four kings, he battled for his natural seed as well as his future spiritual seed—us!

The Four Kings Reveal Four Strategies

By following the steps Abraham took to possess his promises, we gain fresh strategies for the future possession of our own promises. By studying the names of the four kings that Abraham battled in order to save Lot and his family, and by examining the names of each king's dominion (all documented in Genesis 14:9), we gain keen insight into the strategy of the enemy, as well as the strategies we can use to war over our own inheritance and walk forward in faith.

The King of Elam: Chedorlaomer

- *His name* means "to bind sheaves." This implies a "binding up."[1]
- *His dominion* was Elam, which means "eternity."[2]
- *The strategy of the spirit* associated with the king of Elam is to imprison by binding up with cords, or to bind so that one is unable to move forward. This strategy implies that we can be bound to our past, so the enemy uses emotions, fear, sickness and other strongholds to keep us bound. The word "bind" also implies a "bent mind." Some of us are bent in the wrong direction in our thinking concerning God's delivering power and His ability to heal and restore. The enemy desires to keep us "eternally" bound up.
- *Our strategy:* If we rely on our natural senses, natural eyesight and natural understanding, then we will remain bound. It is time to shift into the supernatural!

The King of Nations: Tidal

- *His name* means "terrible, great fear, to make afraid" and to cause to "shrink back and crawl away."[3] Another definition of the name *Tidal* is associated with the word *serpent*, which is another word for divination and witchcraft.[4]
- *His dominion:* He was the king of nations. This implies that this spirit today is a territorial stronghold; it demonically influences large amounts of territory. The word *nations* in this passage refers to not only a people, but it is also used figuratively as a "swarm of locusts" and "to be lifted up."[5]
- *The strategy of the spirit* associated with Tidal attempts to make us so fearful that we shrink back from the warfare needed to win the victory. This is an occult spirit that hides the truth from us so that when we are attempting to see and receive revelation, it is hidden. This stronghold attempts to exalt itself in our eyes. Like a swarm of locusts, it attempts to devour our future if we believe the lies of our enemy.
- *Our strategy:* As we press into the supernatural, we must take care that we do not shrink back in fear! Even though the serpent spirit speaks lies, we must not believe them. We must learn to use supernatural vision and wholeheartedly depend upon the Spirit of God and what He says about our future.

The King of Shinar: Amraphel

- *His name* means "sayer of darkness."[6]
- *His dominion:* Shinar was the ancient name for the territory known as Babylon. The city of Babylon stood on the Euphrates River, and it is believed to be where the Tower of Babel once stood. Like the language of

Babel, the name *Babylon* means "mixed and confused."[7]
Today Babylon is symbolic of the world system. The
spirit encompasses all that is evil upon the earth, especially when referring to the economic system. The
love of money and its evil influence is connected to
the spirit of Babylon.

- *The strategy of the spirit* associated with Amraphel,
  king of Shinar, is to speak darkness over every situation. There will never be any hope in his words. Most
  of us are at war against the evil effects of the Babylon
  spirit. The stronghold is like an octopus, wrapping its
  demonic tentacles around businesses, corporations,
  governments, school systems, churches and families. Not only does the spirit pervert the economic
  system, but it also demonically influences structures
  and governments. This spirit speaks darkness into
  every structure of influence. It has robbed the school
  systems of godly prayer and direction and has murdered innocent children in the medical structures.

- *Our strategy:* Like Abraham, we must cross over into
  warfare against this destructive spirit. Overthrowing
  the influence of this demonic spirit will require words
  of faith and declaring God's life over the death structures it has influenced. Once again, it may appear as if
  we are losing the battle, but with supernatural vision,
  we will see the victory. We must protect ourselves
  by listening only to what God says concerning our
  future.

The King of Ellasar: Arioch

- *His name* means "lion-like."[8]
- *His dominion:* Ellasar was a town in Babylonia; once
  again, it represents the principalities of Babylon. Inter-

estingly, the name *Ellasar* actually translates as "God is the chastener."[9]

- *The strategy of the spirit* associated with the king of Ellasar is to raise his head as a roaring lion that attempts to steal, kill and destroy.

- *Our strategy:* As we cross over into our places of promise, we must not listen to the voice of the enemy. He will attempt to sound like the true roar of the Lion of Judah, but his is a false sound. Although the devil will roar over our circumstances and attempt to cause us to fear and back off from our crossover point, we must cross over on dry land. The Lord has gone before us and has already defeated our enemies! Ultimately, God will chasten our enemies as we cross over into our destiny using our supernatural eyesight. Do not hasten to words you hear in the natural realm. Trust in the Spirit of the Lord!

Do you see how examining their names gives us so much insight into our enemy's strategy? And do you see how we can glean from that insight ways to fight our battles more effectively so that our highway is made less rough? Yes, it is a difficult road to travel, and yes, it is often a road leading into the unknown, but our God gives us the tools necessary to build our character and faith and enable us to walk it in victory.

Now, are you ready to possess some ground in the Spirit? I know you are because you are destined to possess your promises! Let's look at how the sevenfold Spirit of God gives us the fullness necessary to walk even more confidently.

We Need His Sevenfold Spirit

In order to cross over into the unknown and pursue the destiny God has for each of us, we need the fullness of God's Spirit operating in our lives. The book of Isaiah reveals the sevenfold Spirit of God. Let's examine this passage as a foundation for further understanding the seven attributes of His Spirit:

> A shoot will come up from the stump of Jesse; from his roots a Branch will bear fruit. The Spirit of the LORD will rest on him—the Spirit of wisdom and of understanding, the Spirit of counsel and of power, the Spirit of knowledge and of the fear of the LORD—and he will delight in the fear of the LORD. He will not judge by what he sees with his eyes, or decide by what he hears with his ears; but with righteousness he will judge the needy, with justice he will give decisions for the poor of the earth. He will strike the earth with the rod of his mouth; with the breath of his lips he will slay the wicked.
>
> Isaiah 11:1–4

This passage is a prophetic word about the coming of Jesus and the divine attributes He would have. These attributes, outlined in the Isaiah passage, are that the Spirit of the Lord would rest on Him and that He would have wisdom, understanding, counsel, might, knowledge and the fear of the Lord. Because we are one with Christ, each of these attributes is bestowed as a mantle of divine authority upon every believer.

The First Attribute: The Spirit of the Lord Himself

Now, let's look at the first attribute of God that is available to every believer. It is the Spirit of the Lord Himself. This may sound a bit confusing, as we are talking about the attributes of the sevenfold Spirit of God, and the Spirit of the Lord as one attribute sounds redundant. But Scripture is clear that the "Spirit of the Lord" coming down to rest upon a person is an actual gift that God imparts to His chosen ones.

Jesus, the Branch, was a descendant from the root of Jesse. We know that Jesse was David's father and that Jesus was from the lineage of David and Jesse. The name Jesse is translated as "I possess."[10] The spiritual DNA of Christ involved possessing a promise. It is the very same DNA that each of us inherits—a determination and divine grace to possess all that the Father has for us.

Verse 2 states that the Spirit of the Lord rested upon Christ. The word LORD is from the name Jehovah in this passage. *Jehovah* means "the all-existing One." The full translation goes even further to explain that the name also means "to come to pass, to cause to bring about and to happen, and (cause to) come about and to become."[11] In other words, Jehovah is the God of our future! He is not only all-existing, but He also causes our future words and promises to manifest. And along with that is the power to become. Wow! This means that we have been given the power to become the sons and daughters of God and, therefore, to take our rightful place and receive our full inheritance!

So when the Spirit of the Lord (Jehovah) came upon Jesus, a supernatural empowerment rested upon Him to fulfill His destiny. It is the very same with each of us. The same power is given to us to fulfill our future. And because we have received Him, He gave us the "power to become the sons of God":

> He came unto his own, and his own received him not. But as many as received him, to them gave he power to become the sons of God, even to them that believe on his name: which were born, not of blood, nor of the will of the flesh, nor of the will of man, but of God.
>
> John 1:11–13, KJV

Along with that "power to become" is a bestowment of the fullness of God to accomplish whatever is needed for any given situation.

When the Spirit of the Lord comes upon us, we are empowered to do great exploits. His Spirit comes upon us like a mantle of authority and power. The word *upon* actually means for something to come on us to take us "up"! In other words, this part of His character empowers us to come up to another level. Just as heaven comes to earth when we pray, we rise up to meet heaven and come into agreement with His will and Word!

When the fullness of the Spirit of the Lord falls upon us, we can move in the different attributes of His sevenfold Spirit, such as prophecy (revelation), wisdom, might, etc. Scripture gives us vivid examples of the sevenfold attributes of God's Spirit empowering the saints.

When the Spirit of the Lord fell upon King Saul, for example, he prophesied. This happened to Saul two times when he came into the company of prophets. He gained a supernatural ability to receive revelation, to see into the Spirit and to move in a gift of prophecy.

Gideon also was empowered by the Spirit of the Lord to blow the trumpet. Although the people had gathered to put him to death because he had destroyed the altars of Baal, the blowing of the trumpet defeated a death assignment against him. It also released a supernatural sound that gathered an army for war against God's enemies.

The Spirit of the Lord came upon David when Samuel anointed him as the next king: "So Samuel took the horn of oil and anointed him in the presence of his brothers, and from that day on the Spirit of the LORD came upon David in power" (1 Samuel 16:13). From that day on, David was established to be the next king of Israel, and every challenge David faced thereafter prepared him to rule and reign. David was able to defeat Goliath, kill a lion and a bear and lead armies into battle; all because he was under the Spirit of might (one of God's sevenfold attributes). Later, other attributes of God's sevenfold Spirit manifested to empower David, such as the Spirit of counsel and the Spirit of wisdom.

Judges 13:25 describes how the Spirit of the Lord also was upon Samson. He later had supernatural strength under the mantle of His Spirit and His might.

"But we all, with open face beholding as in a glass the glory of the Lord, are changed into the same image from glory to glory, even as by the Spirit of the Lord" (2 Corinthians 3:18, KJV). The Word says that we can have the very same Spirit of the Lord upon us as we are transformed into His image and move from glory to glory! In fact, in order to move from one level of glory to the next level (another crossing over), we need the fullness of the Spirit of the Lord operating in our lives.

It is important to understand that the impartation of the Spirit of the Lord is only the first attribute of the Spirit of God. Now let us examine the other six.

The Second Attribute: The Spirit of Wisdom

During seasons of transition, we have to depend upon God's wisdom. Praying for God's perfect will to be done is important, but we also must pray to receive divine insight and proper spiritual judgment.

The word *wisdom* is a Hebrew word that translates as not only having wisdom, but also being wise and skillful in warfare, administrations and religious affairs.[12] This is exciting because it means we can depend upon God's Spirit of wisdom to teach us the skills we need for spiritual warfare. Going into battle without wise strategy is wasted time and energy, especially in this season. And, after all, who has extra time and energy to be wasted?

Because God's wisdom is different from natural wisdom, we must touch heaven to receive His divine wisdom for our spiritual battles. Otherwise, we are simply "beating the air" with no direction or strategy, about which the apostle Paul speaks (see 1 Corinthians 9:26). Fighting a war with no divine strategy or direction is similar to a boxer beating the air and never striking the opponent. Can you imagine going into warfare and simply waving our arms in the air? How effective would that be? The enemy most likely would be wondering if we would ever throw a solid punch! Precious saints, it is time to touch heaven so we can become effective warriors!

King Solomon is perhaps the best example in the Bible of a man being empowered with God's wisdom and knowledge. Rather than asking for riches, wealth and honor, Solomon asked for wisdom and knowledge so that he could properly judge the people. This pleased the Lord, so He bestowed upon Solomon great wisdom (see 2 Chronicles 1:10–12). God's wisdom instructed Solomon as he built the Lord's temple and later instructed the worship. As we approach the end times, we must receive a greater measure of God's wisdom so that we build our temples to house His glory and so that our worship is led by His Spirit.

The Lord also desires to equip us with His divine administrative skills, which empower our businesses, churches and ministries. In fact, because He is bound to His covenant promises, His heart is to give us everything needed to ensure our success.

As we venture into unknown territory, we cannot depend upon old wisdom that was learned during a past season or else we will be using antiquated weapons. Crossing over into our land of promise requires freshly sharpened weapons. Sharpened spiritual discernment, wisdom and an understanding of the mechanics of spiritual warfare are needed in this season. Depending upon God's Spirit of wisdom ensures our victory in our new places of authority.

The Third Attribute: The Spirit of Understanding

Two attributes of God's Spirit, wisdom and understanding, are closely connected in Scripture. A measure of wisdom and knowledge is needed when the outcome involves understanding. This is why we need the Spirit of wisdom *and* understanding operating in our lives.

To have full spiritual understanding, we must operate in spiritual discernment. Discernment involves a natural ability of understanding; this is referred to as intellect. But we need more than intellectual understanding in this season. If we do not have proper discernment, our understanding will be based upon past knowledge and wisdom. New moves of God's Spirit must be properly discerned so that the fresh move of the Spirit will be understood. Attempting to fully understand without God's dimension of discernment causes us to reason with our intellectual minds only. If we reason with our intellectual nature, we will not understand the spiritual dynamics of all that God is saying and doing. We cannot judge properly with the natural eye because God moves by our faith. Plus, He is doing things behind the scenes that we are unable to see at this time.

God has promised to give us an acuteness of spiritual discernment—the same dimensions that Christ had. Jesus knew when the Pharisees had ulterior motives, and He was empowered to properly judge the motives of others' hearts. He also had the ability to discern the demonic spirits that were operating, and His disciples operated in that same power.

We need this empowerment, as well, and God has promised to equip us with that dimension of His Spirit. As we pray for heaven to come to earth, aligning ourselves with God's perfect will, we need greater measures of spiritual discernment in order to provide us with greater understanding.

The Fourth Attribute: The Spirit of Counsel

The Spirit of counsel is the attribute of God that involves His godly direction and instruction. As most of you know, there is counsel from man and then there is divine counsel, which comes only from the Father. We need both. But there is specific instruction that we receive only when we are in the throne room. Proverbs 19:21 states that although many plans are in a man's heart, only God's counsel will be able to stand and bring forth the fruit that is needed.

Approaching God through an intimate relationship properly positions us to receive His divine direction, correction and instruction. It is in this intimate relationship that He reveals the purpose for His plans, which affects our future. This is where our "whys" get answered. When we struggle with our need to know, our Father overshadows us with so much love and purpose that nothing else matters.

His counsel is similar to a blood transfusion. He counsels and loves us, while providing us with a life-giving transfusion that sets us back on track with our destiny. No longer are we striving to please man. Rather, we rest in His divine direction for our lives. As He counsels, we have renewed purpose and vision, which propel us to achieve our destiny.

"When faced with the destruction caused by the Amalekites, King David sought God's divine counsel for his warfare strategy. David asked the Lord for guidance, and God's answer was to pursue, overtake and recover all (see 1 Samuel 30:8, KJV). In the natural, David might not have been so bold to step out on God's leading. His entire household had been taken by the Amalekites; all the women and children had been taken captive, and the men in his army were ready to stone him. But with the Spirit of God upon him, David followed the Lord's instructions, plundered the enemy's camp and recovered all that was stolen. God's Spirit enabled him to heed the wise counsel of the Lord.

How much we need His divine counsel—especially today! As we move forward, we have to trust in His ability to lead. We are crossing over religious lines of demarcation. Places where we have not ventured have opened, and we have new spiritual trails to follow. We are being commanded to think outside our religious box so that we can move by God's Spirit. If we have ever needed His counsel, dear ones, it is now!

The Fifth Attribute: The Spirit of Might

The word *might* is a Hebrew word which means "strength, valor and bravery." It is further explained as "mighty deeds"![13] How can we possibly do the mighty deeds, or greater things, as Jesus instructed, unless we have the Spirit of might operating in and through us?

The more we pray for heaven to touch the earth, the more we will be challenged with opposition from religious spirits. Religious spirits even hindered Jesus when He was in Nazareth:

> And they took offense at him. Jesus said to them, "Only in his hometown, among his relatives and in his own house is a prophet without honor." He could not do any miracles there, except lay his hands on a few sick people and heal them. And he was amazed at their lack of faith.
>
> Mark 6:3–6

If a religious structure could prevent moves of the miraculous through Christ, just imagine how much these hindering spirits adversely affect our faith today. Pressing past all the religious spirits that hinder the miraculous requires tremendous courage.

As we receive His mantle of might and power, the Lord promises to release His grace. But we must first appropriate the faith needed to receive the strength and courage to operate in the fresh grace He releases. Without the faith to receive His measure of courage, we will not have the full measure of courage that could be appropriated to us.

Right now, with your faith, ask God to release a fresh measure of courage and might. Then, go after those miracles and release heaven's best upon this earth!

The Sixth Attribute: The Spirit of Knowledge

As I began to search for the full interpretation of the word *knowledge*, I was amazed at how often the word *know* was documented. The Lord understands how important it is for us, as humans, to know something—to know our future, to know how, to know what, to know when to acquire knowledge. Knowledge is important so that decisions can be made properly. If we have a fear of failure, we want to know how to do something well. If we have a fear of the future, we seek prophetic insight to gain hope and courage to fulfill our destiny. If we have a fear of death, we search the Word of God and quote Scriptures concerning healing and life. We gain knowledge so that we *know*.

But if we always need to know and we take the wrong road in the knowing process, we can easily open ourselves up to deception and attempts to control our future. How do we do this? By seeking answers from ungodly sources or seeking counselors who will give us the answers we desire to hear. I have witnessed many saints who received godly counsel and godly direction, but it was not the "word" they desired to hear. So, in an attempt to control, they sought counsel that would agree with their decisions and behavior patterns.

We may not always be given insight into a situation. If God is not speaking concerning a certain situation, He is most likely leading us to trust Him in that new season. At this time, we will not "know," but we are still required to trust and follow. Once again, needing to always know will open doors to the voice of the enemy and the occult. Be careful not to fall into this snare of the enemy.

God has promised to mantle us with His Spirit of knowledge. In fact, as He makes Himself "known" to us, He is empowering us with knowledge. As we properly align ourselves with His will and pray that His will be done on earth as it is in heaven, we will be required to know Him at a greater level. As a result, more of His knowledge will be imparted to us. Also, to fully experience a new level of understanding His glory, divine knowledge must be attained. Remember, as the glory is released, we also receive knowledge of the glory of God; this is the reason for this season where heaven invades earth. "For the earth will be filled with the knowledge of the glory of the LORD, as the waters cover the sea" (Habakkuk 2:14).

The tribe of Issachar was gifted with understanding and a knowledge of the times and seasons of the Lord. This is an attribute that each of us can have today. Fully understanding that we live in the end times and knowing our place on the wall will empower us to become effective warriors. Knowing and understanding our times and seasons will empower us to fulfill our prophetic mandates that can be accomplished only in that period of time.

We must fully understand and recognize that God opens doors of opportunity during certain time frames, and these opportunities come and go quickly. The Lord desires to give us what we need as we shift into fruitfulness and fulfillment. As heaven touches earth, expect to become more empowered with His divine knowledge concerning all that concerns you.

The Seventh Attribute: The Fear of the Lord

So we have studied six of the seven attributes of God: the Spirit of God Himself as He comes upon a person to empower him or her, wisdom, understanding, counsel, might and knowledge. The last attribute concerning the sevenfold Spirit of God is the fear of the Lord. The Word states that God did not give us a spirit of fear. Rather, He has given us a spirit of power, love and a sound mind (see 2 Timothy 1:7). Therefore, the fear of the Lord is not the same as the "spirit of fear."

There is a fear that is tormenting, and this fear is from Satan. If you suffer anguish, terror and torment, then there is a demonic assignment targeted toward you. Conversely, there is a fear that is a healthy, reverent awe of God. The Lord will not torment us with fear. The fear of the Lord is being conscious of sin. It is an understanding and awareness of His desire for holiness and righteousness and is concluded with a deep need to repent.

All too often, we take the Lord for granted. During church services, many have abandoned a holy reverence of the Lord's presence. Although we are not to become "spooky spiritual," there is a degree of respect and admiration that should be voluntary when we witness the Lord's anointing and presence. Often I have wondered how we have grieved the Holy Spirit, who has a desire to commune with us. We are His Bride, and He is requiring intimacy, yet we are too preoccupied with how long the services are, what time it is, what we were doing the day before and what we will experience later in the day. We are caught up with the daily cares of life and forget that He is waiting to speak to us. Giving someone time says to that person that he or she is valued. How much do we honestly value the Lord?

If I go for long periods without studying the Word, I become fearful. I am not afraid that I will be punished (this is an unhealthy and unjustified fear), but I am concerned that I will miss out on what He desires to speak. I need my daily manna, a fresh word from Him, so that I am empowered to fulfill His will for my life. If I am not seeking Him daily, then I am taking Him for granted. I need to be in awe of Him.

We also need to be mindful that we are to stand in awe of His marvelous works. Nehemiah 1 speaks of the terribleness of God: "I beseech thee, O Lord God of heaven, the great and terrible God, that keepeth covenant and mercy for them that love him and observe his commandments" (Nehemiah 1:5, kjv). The passage is speaking of this "terrible" attribute in the sense of our having awe and reverence of Him because of the power and might of His character.

It is spiritually healthy to fear the Lord because of His greatness. Aren't you glad that He keeps His covenant with you and promises to show forth His love and mercy? He promises to do this if we are faithful to fulfill our part, which is to love Him and observe His commandments. Becoming fearful of not fulfilling what He requires is a healthy lifestyle that ensures a standard of righteousness we all need.

The aspect of God's Spirit that is the fear of the Lord is needed in this season. If we do not possess a reverential fear, we become easy prey for the enemy. God promises that He will manifest in a greater way, exposing all lack of reverence and respect for His Word and His presence! He promises to keep us tracking on the right road, following the right Spirit—His Holy Spirit—by turning up the fire that keeps us all in line. Aren't you excited He loves us that much?

The Unhealthy Fear of "Not Knowing"

Most of us have failed in our attempt to be led totally by the Spirit of God, especially when we have judged by our natural sight. At times I have gotten in such a spiritual tizzy about the unknown that I actually opened the door to a demonic attack. Were you aware that if we always have to "know" why, where, when and how, and if we are not trusting God and His Word, it releases a witchcraft assignment against us?

The translation of the word *serpent* is linked to the words for "divination" and "the need to know." Most of us are aware that divination satisfies a "need to know." Hopefully we seek the word of the Lord when we need to know His plans for our lives. However, nonbelievers seek out fortune-tellers and spirits of divination to satisfy their need to know. If we become impatient with God's timing and constantly "need to know," then we may be opening a door to divination that releases the assignment of witchcraft against us.

Witchcraft and divination are connected with the occult. The word *occult* means "hidden." The purpose of occult spirits is to keep things hidden from us. The Lord may deliberately hide things from us so that our faith is further developed. If we are constantly murmuring and complaining with a need to know, then the enemy causes a counterattack to keep everything even more hidden. This could be a never-ending cycle if we do not become more alert to the demonic strategies.

Witchcraft and divination assignments manifest in many different ways. In his book *Shadow Boxing*, Dr. Henry Malone describes the different root causes that reinforce demonic entrances into our lives. Some of these roots are independence, rebellion, stubbornness and counsel from mediums, who offer people "answers" when they "need to know" their future.[14] When we do not trust the Lord and are not aligning ourselves with His plan for our lives, we can easily become independent, stubborn and rebellious. We have to train ourselves to not need to know everything ahead of God's time to reveal, and instead move forward in faith and confidence in His ability to direct us.

Check to see if you are dealing with some of these problems. Examine the list below and determine whether or not you have been struggling with these issues and if you are continuing to cycle through these same problems over and over. Place a check beside any items listed that you have had difficulty overcoming.

Anorexia nervosa
Anti-Semitism
Bulimia
Compromise
Confusion
Continuously making wrong decisions
Cults (false doctrines)
Deception
Doubt
False prophets and preachers
False teachers
False tongues
Immaturity
Inappropriate behavior
Intellectualism
Intestinal problems
Irresponsibility
Racism
Sickness
Unbelief

If you checked one or more of these problems, it is possible that your need to know has caused you to move into an area of agreement with the lies of Satan or opened doors to the occult. If you have done so, please do not allow an ungodly fear to torment you. Do not allow a spirit of fear to trouble you if you have not been obedient or have lacked trust in the Lord's direction. If you feel that God is requiring more faith and trust, be careful that you do not remain in a place of needing to know all the details. Simply repent of a constant need to know and a lack of trust in God and close the door to demonic attacks. Begin as Abraham, stepping out and letting go of your past, and move forward in trust.

In other words, it will not look the same as we move into a new arena. The promise is the same, but the circumstances surrounding the promise are different. When we fully depend upon God's Spirit, we will not be able to judge by what we see or hear in the natural. "His delight is in the fear of the LORD, and He shall not judge by the sight of His eyes, nor decide by the hearing of His ears" (Isaiah 11:3, NKJV). If we make decisions based on what we see and hear in the natural, we limit God. Following God requires a greater level of faith. We must develop more mature spiritual senses and spiritual eyesight in order to possess what God has promised us. In order to be on guard and ready, we must learn to depend on the sevenfold Spirit of God. Only by following His direction, using His wisdom and exercising our understanding by the Spirit will we have success and see the fulfillment of God's promises to us.

The Dream of the Higher Highway

I remember complaining to the Lord about faith. One night in my prayers before falling asleep, I began to pour out my heart to the Lord: *Father, I can't seem to walk in the faith that Abraham had. I know I am to walk in faith, but trusting You is too difficult. I am the type of person who needs to be able to see where I am going. I have to know the end result. Taking steps before I fully understand is just too hard!* The Lord answered my complaint with a dream.

I dreamed that my husband, Mickey, and I were traveling in a car down a highway. He was driving. There seemed to be a fog or a mist that hindered my view. We were traveling so fast, and I began to ask Mickey to slow down. I was terrified. Not only was he driving too fast, but I also could not see where we were going. After several pleas, he finally pulled the car to the side and stopped on the highway shoulder. I glanced down and realized we were on a higher level because there was another highway below me. I could see everything down below on the lower highway. But on our higher highway, I could not see.

Then the Lord spoke to me and said that He had placed us on a higher level—a higher way—and that if I really wanted to "see," I could go down to a lower level in the Spirit. If I wanted to remain at this higher level, I would have to trust Him in this new place and develop keener spiritual eyesight. This new level would require a greater understanding of the sevenfold Spirit of God. Praise the Lord that He has promised us His sevenfold Spirit, which empowers us to receive all wisdom and understanding of our times and seasons. We need never to go to any other source but Him to receive all that we need for success in life.

Aligning Our Mission Statement with His

When we align ourselves with Christ's mission statement, then we are fully empowered with every attribute of His Spirit that is needed to fulfill our task. Let's examine His mission and what He was empowered to do:

> The Spirit of the Sovereign Lord is on me, because the Lord has anointed me to preach good news to the poor. He has sent me to bind up the brokenhearted, to proclaim freedom for the captives and release from darkness for the prisoners, to proclaim the year of the Lord's favor and the day of vengeance of our God, to comfort all who mourn, and provide for those who grieve in Zion—to bestow on them a crown of beauty instead of ashes, the oil of gladness instead of mourning, and a garment of praise instead of a spirit of despair.
>
> Isaiah 61:1–3

We are empowered to fulfill the same mission as Jesus. The Spirit of the Lord, therefore, will anoint us to:

- Preach good news to the poor.
- Bind up the brokenhearted.
- Proclaim freedom for the captives.
- Release the prisoners from darkness.
- Proclaim the year of the Lord's favor.
- Proclaim the day of vengeance of our God.
- Comfort all who mourn.
- Give them a crown of beauty instead of ashes.
- Give them the oil of gladness instead of mourning.
- Give them a garment of praise instead of a spirit of despair.

Dear ones, this is the reason we need the Spirit of the Lord in this season! We are crossing over into realms of the supernatural. We are not able to do this mission in our own strength; we need the fullness of the Spirit of the Lord operating within us. We need His divine wisdom, His counsel and direction and the divine knowledge that only He can impart so that we can have victory over the demonic forces that imprison His chosen ones. All of these things are available to each of us as we cross over into a greater level of His glory.

Please pray with me, asking God to forgive you and to empower you with His sevenfold Spirit:

> *Father, I come to You submitting to Your divine plan for my life. I realize that I have attempted to control my destiny and possibly resisted Your plan for my life. I confess that I have sinned in these areas [name the items that you checked], and I repent for opening any doors that allowed the entrance of the occult. I ask forgiveness for not only my sins but also the sins*

*of my ancestors. Thank You for releasing me from any
generational strongholds and ancestral curses that
may have legal entrance into my life. Cleanse me from
all unrighteousness. Thank You for the blood of Jesus
and the awesome completed power of the cross.*

*I ask that You reveal Your sevenfold Spirit to
me. Empower me with Your wisdom, counsel,
understanding and might. I submit my life to the Spirit
of the Lord. You are my God, the God of my life and my
future. I will walk in a reverential fear of the Lord. I
will not judge my circumstances by the natural eye, but
I will trust in Your Word. I choose to align my mission
with Your mission. In Jesus' name I pray, Amen.*

Using Your New Heavenly Strategies

You now have several heavenly strategies to fulfill your
new mission statement.

- After looking once more at Luke 4:18, write down five
  things that you desire to do for the Lord.

  1.

  2.

  3.

  4.

  5.

- Is there someone you know who needs to hear the
  Gospel? Write down his or her name; then write down
  your new strategy as to how you will minister to that
  person.

- Do you have a loved one who is grieving over a death or other loss? Write down the ways in which you could show him or her the love of Christ.

- As you pray, ask the Lord to show you some of your generational (family) strongholds. Before Abraham could "cross over," he went to war. Spend some time with God and get strategies from His throne on how to war for your family so that you all may cross over to the side of victory!

3

Running with the Horses

"If you have run with the footmen, and they have wearied you, then how can you contend with horses? And if in the land of peace, in which you trusted, they wearied you, then how will you do in the floodplain of the Jordan?"

Jeremiah 12:5, NKJV

It was springtime, and all I could think about was being on our school relay team. Anyone who was anyone in our elementary school was part of this spring sports event. If you did not qualify for the six-member track team, you were considered an absolute "nothing." Every morning I would awaken and imagine myself running swiftly toward the finish line.

I had to prepare myself emotionally and physically for the tryouts. I was very small for my age and had short legs, so I had to work extra hard to keep up with the other long-legged fifth graders. I felt that I made three strides for every one of theirs, not to mention the extra breaths I had to take. I remained after school for several weeks practicing my run. I drew a line in the dirt for the finish line and then backed away for at least 75 yards. I practiced hearing the gym teacher shout, "On your mark! Get set! Go!"

I practiced the distance over and over. Finally the preliminary tryouts came. I lined up alongside the other runners. Being the shortest and smallest, I was also the least confident. Although intimidated, I wanted to be on the team so desperately that I was determined to give it my very best effort. The results were not good: I was one of the last to cross the finish line. I left with my head low. It took so long for me to walk home that my parents set out to find me! We had a very long family discussion about being a winner even in defeat, but it did not help.

The actual tryouts were the next day. During the night I had figured out how I would run and win. I decided to take off running before our instructor said "Go!" That way I would have a running start!

It was time to line up for the race. Knowing I could win if I cheated with my planned head start, I was so confident that I stood in the middle of the line. I focused on the finish line and envisioned the trophies, awards and ribbons I would receive as a member of our school relay team.

"On your mark! Get set!" she shouted. Then off I flew with at least a full five-second head start! Before she said "Go!" I was way ahead and strutting—oops, excuse me, I mean "running" strong. I ran with all my might, and yet those other fifth graders still overtook me. But I finished as number five, just barely making it across the finish line to be on the six-person relay team. Even with a five-second head start, I still came in fifth place—that proves how slow I really was!

"I made it! I made it!" I bragged, deceiving myself into thinking I was fast.

"Sandra Kay Davis," my gym teacher called out, "come over here a minute."

Uh-oh, I'm caught, I thought.

"Did you start out before I said go?" she questioned.

"Well, uh, no, I don't think so," I lied, while attempting to look innocent.

"Well, all right then. Good job, Sandra." She walked away, and I became the fifth post runner on the team.

Well, you can imagine what happened. On the day that our team ran, we lost our race. Our principal filmed the relays. As our team later watched the film, my gym teacher said, "Well, it looks as if we began to lose the race along the fifth post." Guess who was on fifth post? I was the runner who slowed down the entire team. We were ahead of the game until they passed the baton to me, and I ran so slowly that the other teams passed me by.

Did I learn my lesson? Well, I still have a lot of ambition, I am still very competitive in sports, and I still like to win. But I no longer cheat to win!

My pace for today's race—the race that God has set before me to fulfill the work He has called me to do in this life on earth—is not based upon my ability to run in the natural. Rather, I have learned to run in the spiritual. I do not want to slow down the Lord's team, so I rely on Him to help me run as fast as necessary to do what He instructs. It is what I refer to as getting a "pace for His race."

A Pace for His Race

Our lives are a race that God has given us to run, not in the physical, but in the spiritual realm. In this Great Race, time is a precious commodity. Have you noticed how it almost always flies by? I often wish I could "buy some time," because there are never enough hours in the day. I also struggle with guilt for all the times in the past when I have made poor decisions and, like a runner in a footrace, lost valuable time or even missed God's timing. Have you felt that way, too? Many of us have struggled with the very same things. But there is hope! We can actually redeem the time that was stolen from us.

One day as I was feeling very sorry for myself for time I had lost, the Lord spoke straightforwardly to me. It was His corrective voice. No matter what spiritual season I am experiencing, His corrective voice always sounds the same, and I recognize it immediately! He said, *Sandie, what are you doing wearing sackcloth and ashes?* His tone alarmed me; it reminded me of my father when I deserved an "I-told-you-so" correction. I visualized God with His arms folded, tapping His foot and expecting me to shift out of my negative attitude. Now I know how Elijah felt when God addressed his doubt and unbelief.

At first, I did not know to what He was referring, and I immediately rose up to defend myself. I must admit I had an attitude as I stood my ground. *Who, me? God, I'm not wearing sackcloth and ashes.*

He answered, *Stop feeling so sorry for yourself! Don't you know there is nothing that I cannot fix for you? I can redeem your time. Did you consider asking Me for what you need?*

I needed that correction. Why did I not believe that God could give me back the time I had lost? I frantically began to search God's Word concerning His ability to redeem my times and seasons. And there it was, in Ephesians 5:15–16: "See then that you walk circumspectly, not as fools but as wise, redeeming the time, because the days are evil" (NKJV).

I got excited as I read these verses. They contained a promise. I could stand on it and believe that God would redeem my time. I repented because I had been foolish and had not walked in His divine wisdom concerning His times and seasons for my life. I also realized that I had allowed the fear of the unknown to hinder my courage to "cross over" into my destiny. I thoroughly investigated other translations, as well as *Strong's Concordance*, and learned that the word *redeem* in this passage meant that Christ could actually make a payment that would recover the lost time and remove me from the power of the enemy who stole times and seasons.[1]

How awesome! With His own blood, Christ had already paid the price required for redeeming my time. Now I could take my seasons in God back; all I had to declare was, "I am taking it back in Jesus' name!"

I know you are excited with me, aren't you? All of us have missed out on our windows of opportunity, our times and seasons to cross over. But God has redeemed the past and is giving us a fresh start to begin again! God promises:

1. When redemption comes (and it has), you have a new chance to make wise and sacred use of every opportunity for doing good.
2. Because it is God's passion to redeem your loss, He also will give you the same zeal and passion to possess it.
3. Your time becomes your own. In other words, the devil is not in control of your times and seasons.

This should convince you that God is very committed to redeeming us from our past mistakes. But if you need even more proof, let me share one more bit of revelation. *Webster's Dictionary* states that the word *time* also refers to "seasons, opportunities and 'proper' seasons."[2] Ecclesiastes 3:1 tells us that God has a set time for every purpose: "To everything there is a season, a time for every purpose under heaven" (NKJV). In other words, heaven's purposes are intended to come to the earth during a certain time and season. If we are following Him and His timetable, we need to be on time. Not late, not early—on time!

Obviously, timing can be everything, especially in the spirit realm. God prophetically plans certain moves of His Spirit, and when His visitations occur, we must be ready. This is why we need to have a pace for the race—we need to align ourselves with heaven. Most of the prophets are aware that God desires to release an open heaven. By this, I mean that God is bringing heaven to earth and is releasing His promises of fulfillment and breakthroughs. We need to be on time. Let's be sure that our pace is aligned with His.

When Joshua was about to lead Israel across the Jordan River, it was the flood season—the most dangerous time to consider crossing over (see Jeremiah 12:5). But God considered the season, not the circumstances. He simply said, "Now!" It was Israel's season of possession, and they were anointed to cross just at that time.

For many of you, the Jordan is in view, and the enemy is whispering lies to you concerning your crossing. I know that voice, too. Let me describe how his voice sounds to me when I must decide whether or not to cross to the other side and experience victory:

- "If you cross over into the unknown, the giants will kill you!"
- "You are not strong enough to cross over now; even if God tells you to, you won't make it to the other side."
- "Surely that prophet 'missed it' when he said to cross over now. Maybe you need a second opinion."
- "What if you cross over only to find that you missed God's timing again? You'd better not cross over at all!"
- "That is the dumbest thing you have ever thought of doing!"

Running the Race Requires Change

In order to run God's race, we must align with the timing of His Spirit or realize that we are behind schedule. Windows of opportunity are opening supernaturally because we have been knocking on heaven's door. If we ask for His presence, God opens the door wide for us to enter into a new realm of His glory. "Ask and it will be given to you; seek and you will find; knock and the door will be opened to you" (Matthew 7:7).

But as we seek more of His glory, He requires more change! To remain in the race, we must recognize that the Church is in the midst of great transition and obtain a vision for the future.

We have heard it said for years, "The Church will not look the same ten years from now." I first heard that declaration almost two decades ago, and I have not yet witnessed enough of the outward change of the Church. In many ways, the Church still looks the same, and it is because we are not willing to change. Each of us has a tendency to hold onto the past because of our fears of the future and the unknown.

We stubbornly place a steel master lock on our past because it is more comfortable. Maybe you have felt as I have concerning the "letting-go" part—at least we know what to expect if we do the same things the same old way. We will not change because we do not know what else to do. It is very difficult to let go of what is comfortable, such as singing the same songs, preaching the same messages and ordering the church services in the same manner. Even more of a concern is that the ones attempting to fully move with His Spirit are being persecuted so much that they are struggling to hold onto anything! Persecution is the result of a demonic retaliation for moving forward into God's plans for us. Our enemy hates the fact that we are transitioning into greater realms of His glory and, therefore, targets us for destruction. The devil does not want any of us to understand the fullness of the Kingdom message, and those of us who are attempting to fully follow God's Spirit are on the enemy's hit list.

Beloved, we will never embrace change unless we can let go of the past. In order to experience the outward manifestation, we must first open ourselves to "inward" change. Precious saints, please hear me! Bravehearts run with the horses at God's pace, and they know when it is time to embrace the "new thing."

Following are a few questions to help you assess where you are with letting go of the past and ushering in the new thing God has for you within the Body of Christ:

1. Are you trying to follow God's Spirit? *Yes?*
2. Are you trying to follow God with your whole heart and every fiber of your being? *Yes.*
3. Are you feeling lost, isolated and extremely persecuted?
4. Are you frustrated with the religious status quo? *Y*
5. Are you dry, thirsty and filled with a need to see and experience change? *Y*
6. Are you finding yourself challenged by God to let go of the past and move forward?

Dear one, if you answered yes to any of these questions, most likely you are in the midst of transition. God is shifting you out of an old place and into a new place, and He is spiritually preparing you to walk into your new measure. It is your season to walk into your new portion. But don't simply walk—*run* toward your future. There is much to do for the Kingdom of God!

I have often heard the expression that the only difference between a casket and a rut is that a rut has the ends kicked out. Remaining in an old place, a rut, will cause a death structure to be built around you. God does not intend to leave you hopeless and barren. He cares for you so much that He will not allow you to remain in an old rut. He is going to break you out of old patterns of behavior that limit and restrict your growth.

Your New Military Assignment: To Run with the Horses

In Jeremiah 12, the prophet begins to complain about the lack of godliness, with the wicked prospering, declining morals and rebellion being at an all-time high:

> Righteous are You, O LORD, when I plead with You; yet let me talk with You about Your judgments. Why does the way of the wicked prosper? Why are those happy who deal so treacherously? You have planted them, yes, they have taken root; they grow, yes, they bear fruit. You are near in their mouth but far from their mind. But You, O LORD, know me; You have seen me, and You have tested my heart toward You. Pull them out like sheep for the slaughter, and prepare them for the day of slaughter. How long will the land mourn, and the herbs of every field wither? The beasts and birds are consumed, for the wickedness of those who dwell there, because they said, "He will not see our final end."
>
> "If you have run with the footmen, and they have wearied you, then how can you contend with horses? And if in the land of peace, in which you trusted, they wearied you, then how will you do in the floodplain of the Jordan?"
>
> Jeremiah 12:1–5, NKJV

I have to admit, I really cannot blame Jeremiah for his attitude and discouragement. Jeremiah had a ministry call that was unenviable. He survived the reign of five different kings who were all dedicated to idol worship, loose morals and lifestyles with rebellious streaks that would make many of our modern-day presidents appear to be saints.

After Jeremiah pours out to God some of his complaints and questions, God answers Jeremiah with a question.

Don't you just hate it when people do that? Actually, it is an intelligent maneuver, as it puts the ball right back into an opponent's court. Jesus later used this skillful tactic when challenged by the Pharisees, and it totally dumbfounded their evil schemes to discredit the integrity of Christ. Although Jeremiah was not actually an opponent of God, God answered him with the same words He uses with us today: "If you are having trouble at this level, then what are you going to do at a higher level?"

God was now dealing with Jeremiah's mind-set. He was shocking him into a paradigm shift—a change in his thought patterns. Jeremiah had limited thinking concerning his natural abilities. Jeremiah could not see himself rising to a higher level of running at full speed. He was conditioned in his spirit to be a footman.

Footmen cannot see beyond what is directly in front of them. Their vision is blocked by obstacles—problems, negativity and challenges—that stand in their paths; thus, they move slowly on foot. Upon a horse, however, not only does one move faster, but the view is also broader and not so restricted. Jeremiah had survived at a footman's level for a very long season and was remaining there. God was prophesying to Jeremiah and speaking to his potential to rise up and run with the horses!

If we remain on a footman's level, we will see things only through a footman's view. When God begins to renew our minds, He removes old paradigms because they limit our thinking. Paradigms box us into old patterns and mind-sets that prohibit change.

When the Lord says it is time for us to run with the horses, He is saying that it is time for promotion. Get ready to change, to rise up and embrace a new level of maturity and to conquer whatever stands in your way!

Running with Horses Requires Maturity

My husband and I served as pastors of a local church for over fourteen years. Many saints in our church were hungry for God and desired to witness the miraculous and to remain in His presence. But all too often, many of them remained at the footman's level because they focused on ground-level concerns.

Footmen murmur and complain. They focus on the air-conditioning in the church, whether it is too hot or too cold, how the pastor is dressed, if they received enough recognition or how well the church is landscaped.

Those running with the horses do not have the time to be overly concerned about such trivial matters. Running with horses requires a fast pace, a higher level, a higher highway. Running with the horses requires maturity.

Running with Horses Requires the Eye of the Spirit

Running with the horses requires that one see beyond obstacles that block the paths to victory and, more importantly, see through the obstacles to the other side. Horsemen realize that on the other side of the mountain lies victory. On the other side of the river is the possession of the promise. We need a divine ability to see by His Spirit.

We all are in a season when we cannot judge things by our natural eyes. The new level involves depending on God's Word. In my dream of the higher highway, God was showing my husband and me that we needed to come up to a higher level. It had been a long season of battling natural circumstances, and God was requiring that we be led totally by His Spirit. This meant that we could not always "see" where we were going. We could no longer judge by what we saw in the natural, but we had to depend upon our spiritual eyes.

Wow! This is an awesome thought! The Word says that we are seated in heavenly places and are destined to rule and reign with Christ. To do so, we must be led fully by His Spirit.

Developing Spiritual Eyesight

Developing spiritual eyesight requires a new dependence on God's Spirit. Embracing His sevenfold Spirit empowers us to trust Him as we move forward. In order to witness His perfect will on earth—what I refer to as heaven touching earth—we must respond to His direction with greater levels of faith. This requires moving beyond old comfort zones, past doubt and unbelief, and venturing into the unknown. We also must be willing to face the reality that some others may not desire to change; yet we must move forward.

All through his life, Jeremiah travailed with a message to a stubborn, rebellious generation. Jeremiah was called from the womb to be a prophet. He prophesied faithfully for over fifty years, ministering God's words. His entire message focused on repentance and eternal judgment. Remember, he actually lived through the reign of five different kings without witnessing any change at all. Throughout his prophetic ministry, there were no signs of change and no repentance, and in fact, everything was getting worse. Can you possibly imagine how difficult it would be to preach to a group of rebellious people for over fifty years? Can you imagine the heartache Jeremiah felt as God addressed his mind-sets? I would not want a call like Jeremiah had, would you? Talk about a wilderness experience!

But I am convinced that a prophetic voice is perfected in the wilderness. Jeremiah had to develop spiritual eyesight in order to step up to the higher way to which God was calling him.

John the Baptist was another voice that cried out in the wilderness. As he waited for the Messiah, his message burned in his spirit while he echoed "Repent!" over a period of years. Like Jeremiah, John the Baptist also had the endurance needed for the long haul because his wilderness experience gave him the ability to see through spiritual eyes. Although we may feel we have a lot to say, it is only through wilderness experiences that our spiritual insight is heightened.

Patterns of Self-Pity

God's answer to Jeremiah was to jerk him out of his pity-party attitude. Let's face it: We all can get stuck there! Self-pity slows down our pace because we focus on our losses rather than on seeing God's purposes and intended results. Self-pity blames God for losses and makes us bitter and self-focused.

God responded to Jeremiah, "Well, if troubles and challenges overtake you at the footman's level, what will you do when you get promoted? Or, do you even want to be promoted?" (see Jeremiah 12:5, paraphrased).

We must remind ourselves that our view is limited and narrow. We quickly respond to challenges with human reasoning and lessons learned from past experiences. This is why we must renew our minds.

God, on the other hand, sees the bigger picture. He views us from a completed place. He does not need to see things develop before He can understand them. He just speaks it and expects it to happen because He is God. The problem is that we have problems seeing what He sees.

I am reminded also of Joseph, who was sold into slavery. God used Joseph's imprisonment to help establish a seven-year plan to preserve Israel. While Joseph was believing God to help him out of his bleak situation, God was somewhere in Joseph's future working it all out.

It was the same for Jeremiah. God spoke to Israel's future the entire time that Jeremiah ministered. God's only answer to Jeremiah was to get over it and get ready to run with the horses, but all the while God was speaking to Israel's future.

God saw the bigger picture. He was preparing Jeremiah for the worst-case scenario: a faster pace, more pressure, more disasters and a much more difficult and unpredictable terrain. Talk about an instant need to renew your mind to the Word of the Lord!

Don't Go Back!

Going through times of transition and adjusting our pace in His race always tempts a person to "go back." Don't! Has the Lord spoken to you concerning your breakthroughs and told you it was time to "run with the horses"? Don't be tempted to be a footman again.

Let's look again at what it means when God instructs us to run with the horses.

1. You are stronger.

You are not released to move into the place where you run with the horses until you have defeated the enemy at ground level. Ground level is when you are at a level of gaining understanding, gathering revelation and warring with that level of revelation. While in this place of training, the Holy Spirit instructs us concerning our weapons of spiritual warfare, and especially who we are in Him. Self is sanctified, holiness is encouraged and we become worshipers. When we are true worshipers, the Lord of Hosts arises in our situations and begins to defeat our enemies. We overcome our enemies with the blood of the Lamb, the word of our testimony and loving not our lives unto death. Priorities are reevaluated and our hearts are tested to see if we can enter into a new level of possession and anointing.

2. The plumb line has dropped—you passed the test!

A plumb line is dropped, and all things are pulled to that line to measure righteousness and holiness. This is because we are becoming seated in heavenly places with Him. Anointing and authority increase when we achieve this position in Christ. Our prayers become more effective as we pray with greater authority, demons are cast out upon command and we begin to see the establishment of His Kingdom in our hearts and surroundings.

Remember God's answer to Jeremiah: "If you have run with the footmen, and they have wearied you, then how can you contend with horses? And if in the land of peace, in which you trusted, they wearied you, then how will you do in the floodplain of the Jordan?" (Jeremiah 12:5, NKJV). On a positive note, the Lord is saying, "Expect to see much more victory. You have not even begun to see My hand move in power!" Let's begin to expect dynamic breakthroughs. Hallelujah!

3. You are empowered to contend.

On the other hand, the Lord is saying that in order to truly run with a greater strength and to keep up with the horses, we will have to contend with the horses. This means "to burn, be kindled, to glow with anger, zealous, to rival and become angry."[3] God is stirring us with a righteous indignation to destroy all that is hindering our commitment to the Kingdom of God being established upon this earth. We must become so angry with the old patterns, the old lifestyles and the "old things" that we battle with a greater determination than ever before. The Jeremiah passage is also saying that we have been asking God to run with the horses, but we are unwilling to put those old things under our feet, so how can we expect to run with the horses unless we truly *contend* with them?

4. It is your crossing-over time.

When Israel crossed over the Jordan, the river was raging. The waters were dangerous and swift. In the natural, those waters appeared too dangerous for the people to cross. Fear always attempts to gain a foothold at a cross-over point! But Jeremiah 47:2–3, 6–7 says that when Israel defeated the Philistines, there was a sound of the strong horses' stamping hooves:

> This is what the LORD says: "See how the waters are rising in the north; they will become an overflowing torrent. They will overflow the land and everything in it, the towns and those who live in them. The people will cry out; all who dwell in the land will wail at the sound of the hoofs of galloping steeds, at the noise of enemy chariots and the rumble of their wheels. Fathers will not turn to help their children; their hands will hang limp. . . .
> "'Ah, sword of the LORD,' you cry, 'how long till you rest? Return to your scabbard; cease and be still.' But how can it rest when the LORD has commanded it, when he has ordered it to attack Ashkelon and the coast?"

The Philistines are symbolic of the old thing. Their name even means "to wallow in the mud,"[4] pointing to defilement and stagnation. If we are unwilling to cross into our new place, we risk wallowing in the muddy places, which is defilement from unclean spirits.[5] Dear ones, we must rise up and put those seducing spirits under our feet so that we can move forward.

Must the Horse Be Tall?

Are you ready to leave the footmen behind, climb up on that big horse and run? I have found myself asking, *How about a Shetland pony, God?* They are closer to the ground, but I can still leap to the higher level—and I can easily maintain a feeling of control with this smaller animal.

I have never done well with horses. I have fallen off, broken bones, sprained ankles and thus suffered the consequences of attempting to ride. In the natural I would rather remain on foot. But spiritually speaking, a fear of the past hinders our commitment to rise up to a new level. Riding a Shetland pony is definitely a "small step" in the right direction. It will be a rung on the spiritual ladder to your destiny. But have you ever seen a movie in which the mighty warrior rides a Shetland? No! Warriors always ride massive horses so their opponents cannot reach them, spear them or otherwise harm them. Their horses are strong, swift and intimidating to their opponents.

Riding a Shetland is too small a step to be protected from your enemy, as well as to be effective for the Kingdom. We must take the plunge and lock fully into our next season to become empowered as we shift into our new place. By being fully determined, we will become divinely empowered to achieve our destiny in the new place God has for us.

What About the Thickets That Await Us?

I once had the most hardheaded and stubborn horse. She would never mind the restraint of the bit. She would run so fast that I would almost fall off, and then she would come to a sudden halt, hurling me into a thicket. I do not do well with thorns!

This is certainly not my idea of running with the horses. But the warfare will be more intense at this next level. We must not be afraid of the thickets that might await us.

Hinds' Feet for Those "Higher Places"

I am only five feet three inches tall. No wonder I would rather ride a Shetland pony! Besides the fact that they appear safer to me, they are easier for me to mount. I do not even need a saddle with a small pony. I can be confident in my ability to ride bareback. During my 4-H days, riding bareback was quite an accomplishment. Others prided themselves on their ability to hurl themselves up onto their horses, while I could barely jump five inches into the air. I wish I had known the Scripture that states God will give us hinds' feet for those "high" places (see Psalm 18:33). After all, a high place could be anywhere, right?

Running with the horses requires that we develop those hinds' feet—so we can jump on a horse quickly, if needed, sometimes even bareback.

Come On! Cross on Over!

In this season, expect a shift in your pace. Time will go faster, and challenges will be more difficult. But, oh, the sweet taste of great success! God will pour out more grace, more anointing and more strategy in this next season than ever before. Once we have shifted into a place of promised victory, there is no room for backing up!

We will be:

B older
R ighteous
A nointed
V ictorious
E mpowered
H oly
E nthusiastic
A wesome
R esult-oriented
T imely
S anctified

BRAVEHEARTS!

You are empowered with strength to run with the horses and cross over into your land of promise. As you run with the horses, the sound of their hooves will terrify your enemy. Each of us must begin to expect the sword of the Lord to defeat our enemies as we cross over into this new place of possession. His sword will not be quiet until He has accomplished all He has promised.

There are more for you than against you. I am asking the Lord to open your eyes so that you can see God's promises prevailing over your circumstances.

> Father, in the mighty name of Jesus, I ask for a fresh vision for Your children. Lord, give each of us eyes to see and ears to hear what You are speaking in this hour. This is not a season to back away, but a season to press forward! The enemy has attempted to intimidate many of us and seduce us to believe his lies, but we are asking that You empower us with a

vision of breakthrough and destiny. We want to run with the horses and defeat our enemies. We thank You, in faith, for our breakthroughs and for our crossing over into our Promised Land. In Jesus' name, Amen!

7/28/08

4

RESISTING RELIGIOUS PARADIGMS

And Zacharias said to the angel, "How shall I know this? For
I am an old man, and my wife is well advanced in years."

Luke 1:18, NKJV

One day during a church service, the Lord spoke to me
and said, *Sandie, do you really want all that I have for you?*
Well, I could not believe He had asked me that question!
Didn't He know I had laid down my life for the ministry?
Didn't He remember how I had sacrificed my time and
energy to fulfill His will and His purpose for my life? I
felt insulted at first and wondered why He would even
question if I wanted everything He desired to do in me
and through me.

Boldly, I responded straightforwardly: *Of course! Just tell
me what to do, and I will do it! Just ask me to do anything!*

He replied, *I want you to jump in the River.*

Okay! I gladly responded. *This is going to be easy*, I thought.
I have done this before. So I began to jump around physically

in one spot. Then I began to venture out a few feet, still jumping. I knew the next step was to signal to our worship leader that it was time to sing the song "Jump in the River." This was a surefire way to get the entire congregation jumping with me. Soon the whole congregation was jumping. It was fun!

Then the real test came. *That's not all*, He said. *I do not want you just jumping around like you are in the River; I really want you in the River—completely!*

I am, Lord! Look at me now—I am swimming in the water! I began to make arm motions as if I were swimming, throwing one hand in front the other and then swimming backward. Again the congregation joined me. All the people were diving and swimming with their body language. *This is great. Look, Lord, we are all in Your River!*

Then I heard a voice I did not recognize. I thought at first it was my own voice talking. But then I realized it was God's voice speaking to me in an unfamiliar way. I now refer to this as His "transition voice." God sounds different during times of transition. He requires us to hear Him and know Him in an entirely new way. He desired a new response from me, and it was not in simple hand-and-foot maneuvers. It would require a complete paradigm shift in the way I understood His Kingdom message. I would have to come out from established mind-sets and old religious thinking and embrace His new wine.

Jumping into His River required many different changes. God began to require that I minister differently—preach differently and even prophesy differently. He was taking me to an entirely new level. The ministry time was more anointed and more powerful than ever before, yet still it was hard to leave the old, comfortable way of doing things. In fact, I became so uncomfortable with the changes that I began to step backward and resist the new assignments He gave me. Then one night I had a startling dream.

God Laid Open My Mind

I have had so many mind-sets concerning God and what He is saying that He often has to knock me out at night and speak to me in my dreams. That way I cannot argue with Him and dispute what He asks me to do! For people who argue with God—and we all do—dreams and visions are a method of communication God uses to bypass our natural thinking and convey His will and purposes to us.

God used a dream to change my mind—literally. He wanted me to get out of my comfort zone, to resist the religious paradigms I was used to and to follow His will instead of my own—all for the benefit of the Body of Christ.

I dreamed that an axe fell from heaven and split my head wide open. Yes, you read that right! God split my mind wide open with heaven's axe, which lays open every mind-set and chops that mind-set to the root. It was not a gory dream. There was no blood, and it really sounds much worse than it was. God had to get my attention, however, and this dream certainly did that.

As my mind was laid wide open, two clothespins fell from heaven, and God's hands used them to pin back my brain on each side. In the natural, clothespins hang clothes out to dry. But in my dream I was the one being hung out to dry, in the sense that I was being directed to remain open-minded concerning everything He told me to do.

God said, *Sandie, I am going to clip your mind back so that you have to remain open-minded concerning My River and all that I tell you to do. If you want to be led by My Spirit, you will have to allow Me to shift you out of your stinking thinking. Your thought patterns and religious structures are limiting how I want to move through you.*

When I awoke from the dream, I fully understood the interpretation. I had resisted His instructions because His new direction did not fit into my religious box. I had limited Him and how He desired to move in our church services because it did not fit into our structure. Although my husband and I felt that we were very open to His Spirit, we both had old belief systems concerning moves of His Spirit. Now God was saying that we must get the anointing out of the box and that I was to remain open-minded.

The Zacharias Lesson

God will use whatever means necessary to get us out of the box and deliver us from limited thinking. As I stated, He often uses dreams and visions to bypass our minds and plant a Holy Spirit computer chip of instruction and wisdom into our brains while we sleep. Most likely God has already been speaking to each of you concerning changes He desires for you to embrace as you move forward by His Spirit.

Sometimes God even sends an angel to speak to us, if necessary. Remember Zacharias? He argued with Gabriel when the angel brought him a message from God. Can you even begin to imagine someone having the boldness to argue with an angel who stands in the very presence of God?

Zacharias was no different than most of us. He was just going about his daily routine. Can't you just picture him in the temple, fulfilling his daily responsibilities, doing the nine-to-five routine, business as usual? I am sure the barrenness he and Elizabeth had experienced was heavy upon his heart, but the Scripture does not indicate that Zacharias was doing anything out of the ordinary when Gabriel appeared. He was not in an intimate prayer time interceding for his wife, Elizabeth, and her inability to conceive a child. But the angel appeared and spoke: "Do not be afraid, Zacharias, for your prayer is heard; and your wife Elizabeth will bear you a son, and you shall call his name John" (Luke 1:13, NKJV).

Well, this rocked Zacharias's boat! Zacharias was not like Peter, who could not wait to walk on water at the bidding of the Lord. Instead of receiving the promise of a son by faith, Zacharias began to confront the angel and explain all the reasons why it was impossible:

> And Zacharias said to the angel, "How shall I know this? For I am an old man, and my wife is well advanced in years." And the angel answered and said to him, "I am Gabriel, who stands in the presence of God, and was sent to speak to you and bring you these glad tidings. But behold, you will be mute and not able to speak until the day these things take place, because you did not believe my words which will be fulfilled in their own time."
>
> Luke 1:18–20, NKJV

Zacharias was experiencing a mind-set problem when the angel announced that what had been impossible would now become possible. His mind-set limited God's ability and desire to heal his wife from the curse of barrenness. She had been barren for many years, and now she was too old to have children. Zacharias's response indicated that surely God knew she was simply too old to have a child now. After all, having kids at that age was ridiculous! I often wonder what would have been Zacharias's response if he had talked to Abraham and Sarah and met their miracle baby.

As a result of Zacharias's doubt and unbelief, the angel struck him dumb. Zacharias was unable to speak until his son, John the Baptist, was born. To ensure that no negative speech would negate the fruitfulness of the promise, Zacharias would have no input until the time of fulfillment.

How sad that Zacharias had to learn such a hard lesson. I know for a fact that it would almost destroy me if I were unable to talk for nine months. I once had laryngitis, and my physician's prescription was for me not to talk for five days. I almost went crazy because I like to talk—I mean, I *really* like to talk! I only lasted three days, and then I caved in and talked up a storm.

The Children of Israel and Paradigm Shifts

Actually, three days is about the time of a human's endurance for most things. After that, it becomes very difficult to remain on track. It seems that at times we all have a short fuse when it comes to a challenge. Whether we face a test of faith, of obedience or of patience and endurance, it is just downright hard to maintain a good attitude and respond properly.

Remember the children of Israel? Only three days after they crossed over the Red Sea, they began to backslide. Three days without water, and they decided that life was too difficult and they could not trust God for their provision. They blamed their problems on Moses and then wanted to go back to Egypt. It is the same for us today. We get "tanked up" on Sunday, and by Wednesday—three days later—we begin to leak!

The problem with the Israelites was that they had a mind-set concerning how God spoke to them. Remember that in times of transition, God speaks differently. While they were in Egypt, God spoke to them by promising a deliverer. At the sign of their first challenge, they decided that Moses was not capable of leading, so they wanted to elect a new deliverer. Surely, they thought, God would answer their prayers by providing another leader. God, however, was speaking differently in their transition. God desired to prove Himself to the Israelites by performing a miracle. God had Moses throw a piece of wood into the bitter waters, and the waters were made sweet:

Then Moses led Israel from the Red Sea and they went into the Desert of Shur. For three days they traveled in the desert without finding water. When they came to Marah, they could not drink its water because it was bitter. (That is why the place is called Marah.) So the people grumbled against Moses, saying, "What are we to drink?"

Then Moses cried out to the LORD, and the LORD showed him a piece of wood. He threw it into the water, and the water became sweet.

There the LORD made a decree and a law for them, and there he tested them.

Exodus 15:22–25

You see, the Israelites had a mind-set of how God should speak. They limited Him to how He cared for them in their old season. The Lord desired to prove Himself as a miracle-working God whom they could trust. God wanted His children to follow Him wholeheartedly and to believe that whatever He promised, He was well able to perform.

Both Zacharias and the camp of Israel were challenged to embrace a paradigm shift. God was introducing a new paradigm that would shift them out of an old, limiting mind-set that concerned God performing His perfect will. God desired to bring heaven's purpose to the earth and bless His children. He desires to do the very same for us, and He will do so if we respond properly and make a shift into great faith. God will bring heaven's plans, His perfect will made manifest on earth, if only we will shift with Him.

Beloved, God desires to shift us out of old patterns of doubt and unbelief. He wants to deliver us from all our barren situations!

Paradigms Defined

We have been tossing around this word *paradigm*. But what exactly is a paradigm?

A paradigm is a mental structure that limits us. It can be a very rigid, stiff and legalistic way of thinking. A paradigm involves our thought patterns, reasoning and ways of thinking. It is a mind-set based on human reasoning and old behavior patterns. Many times a paradigm is negative and, therefore, limits us from believing things can be different. This is the reason so many of us resist change; when something new is offered, we respond negatively because we are afraid of alterations in our lifestyles and belief systems. A religious paradigm keeps us locked into certain religious systems that promote old beliefs and patterns of behavior. When we operate in a religious paradigm, we do not allow ourselves to think outside the box, and we limit God.

Remaining in an old religious structure limits our faith and hope. If God desires to heal someone, for example, we may lock into the way we believe He should heal, and then we miss how God desires for us to pray or minister for that person's healing. What if God desired to heal someone through the skill of a surgeon's hand? If we limit God and believe that He does not use doctors for healing, we might miss His divine plan. If someone believes for a miracle, does that mean a miracle will not occur because he had to endure medical surgery? It is the Lord who is the Healer; a surgeon only has natural skills. But *Jehovah Rapha*, our Healer, is the Lord who performs the healing.

John 5 describes a perfect example of someone who was challenged with a paradigm shift. A man who had suffered with a spirit of infirmity for 38 years lay beside the Pool of Bethesda, hoping that someday someone would place him in the waters of healing. Jesus stopped and asked him, "Do you want to get well?" (verse 6). The man's immediate response was saturated with all types of excuses as to why he could not be healed. "The sick man answered Him, 'Sir, I have no man to put me into the pool when the water is stirred up; but while I am coming, another steps down before me'" (verse 7, NKJV). Jesus replied, "Rise, take up your bed and walk" (verse 8, NKJV). Jesus was ready to heal him at that very instant. But the man had a mind-set. He believed that first an angel had to come to stir up the waters. And he thought that the only way for him to be healed was to be picked up and placed in the water before anyone else got there. His mind-set limited the power of Jesus. Jesus wasn't even going to use the pool as part of the healing, but this man believed that being placed in the water was his only hope.

How many of us have a mind-set as to how we are made whole? What are we waiting for? Are we not receiving our healing because we believe we need visitations from angels? Do we believe we need to see Jesus face-to-face before His healing power can transform our lives? Do we limit God's ability to heal us and restore us? In order to embrace our new season of increased faith, we must not limit God.

Paradigms in our thinking processes resist any type of change. Change, therefore, first must occur in us to make the shift into God's "new thing."

John the Baptist Preached a Paradigm Shift

The very first book of the New Testament confronts us with a paradigm shift. A new message was being presented through John the Baptist. Maybe you have not seen John the Baptist as a pioneer who introduced a new belief system, but he did.

After Malachi, the last book of the Old Testament, the New Testament begins, and it is a radical change. It is a prime example of leaving the "old" and embracing the "new." We are suddenly instructed to embrace a new covenant, a new way and a new understanding of our relationship with God.

Shifting into Kingdom mentality requires leaving the past behind, getting out of the box and being open-minded to a new way of approaching God.

John the Baptist's voice in the wilderness introduces us to a new message—the Kingdom message. He preached a message of fire and repentance. His theology challenged everyone, especially the religious leaders, to repent from their religious traditions and mind-sets and to embrace a new lifestyle. He spoke directly and radically to the sins of King Herod and to the pride and arrogance of the Pharisees. John the Baptist exposed a legalistic religious structure that opposed the Good News of Christ Jesus. John's message directly confronted and challenged the religious culture of the times.

John preached that it was not through religious works, family heritage or religious tradition that one would experience the Kingdom of heaven. Many, especially the religious authorities, opposed this theology and questioned his teachings. John's new teachings directly confronted their beliefs and lifestyles. This was such a new way of thinking that it completely puzzled the Pharisees. They were being challenged to receive revelation by the Spirit of God rather than by their natural minds. All of their lives the Pharisees had studied the law and prided themselves on their relationship with God through their religious deeds. Why shift out of the old when they had it all figured out?

Jesus challenged the religious system with the same fortitude as John the Baptist. He boldly addressed the Pharisees as He introduced the Kingdom message. Jesus added to His daily itinerary many miracles, signs, wonders and deeds that directly opposed the Law. He deliberately healed on the Sabbath, knowing that the religious structure of His time would resist Him. Working on the Sabbath, raising the dead, casting out devils—let me remind you that this did not occur in the Old Testament!—and forgiving sins were only a few demonstrations of His credibility as the Son of Man and the Son of God. He shook paradigms of holiness by declaring "clean" what was once called "unclean." He rocked their religious boats by eating with sinners and making disciples of the city's tax collectors. (That would be like asking an unsanctified IRS agent to minister on our church ministry teams!) He refused to stone an adulteress even though the Law required such punishment. He was not legalistic, and He had compassion for sinners. Jesus was constantly doing the will of the Father, yet He resisted the religious system and the laws men had attached to it.

Jesus did not fit into the paradigm of the old religious structure. He repeatedly and deliberately provoked others so they would be challenged to think differently. He introduced a new way of thinking—a paradigm shift—and a new understanding of the Kingdom of God manifested upon the earth.

All New Revelation Resists Paradigms

All new revelation resists the old paradigms. When the modern prophetic ministry was birthed in 1980, it shook the religious system. I was attending the Christian International Conference when the prophetic movement was birthed, and it was one of the most powerful services I have ever attended. Since that time, God has been imparting His prophetic insight to many prophetic people, and they are moving forth with a strong prophetic revelation.

Many church leaders labeled this movement as heresy and negated the significance of the prophetic ministry. Even though Scripture says we are to covet the gift of prophecy (see 1 Corinthians 14:39), many were opposed to this teaching and ministry. As the Holy Spirit released His voice through the mouths of prophets, the persecution became more and more intense.

Our Savior faced the same opposition. He was obedient to the Father to do everything His Father asked Him to do. Jesus brought heaven to earth as He did the Father's will upon this planet. Yet the people opposed Him.

It is difficult for many of us to admit this, but so often we resist a new move of the Holy Spirit because of our mind-sets. The Holy Spirit is introducing His new wine, a fresh River of power, but because we have mind-sets as to how He moves, we are not open-minded. We easily make the same mistakes as the Pharisees who negated the ministry of Christ.

As Jesus taught His disciples to pray, we are to pray the same today. Our prayer is for the will of the Father to become manifest on this earth—heaven touching earth! The message of the Kingdom is given by Jesus Christ through His prayer, which is documented in Matthew 6: "This, then, is how you should pray: 'Our Father in heaven, hallowed be your name, your kingdom come, your will be done on earth as it is in heaven'" (verses 9–10).

We cannot trust ourselves in this season when God is pouring out His Spirit on all flesh. We must depend totally upon the voice of the Holy Spirit and see with spiritual eyes, as the Father brings His Kingdom to earth.

Radical Behavior Is Required!

Resisting paradigms requires radical behavior! This does not imply that one should be unstable or "weird." But it does mean that in order to shift out of an old paradigm, we must be brave, bold and adamant in servanthood for the Lord. We are not to throw away all accountability with our new radical behavior. In fact, we are to become even more accountable and submitted to godly authority and to His Word.

Jesus was radical and was labeled a heretic and false prophet. He was a revolutionary who led a revolution. He introduced a new paradigm wherever He taught. He was persecuted and rejected—and that very same persecution might also happen to each of us. But I would rather follow Him than pursue a religious structure that limits Him.

Releasing Control

After my dream of God laying the axe to the root of my religious spirit, things changed in our church. When my husband and I began to back away from the way we thought God wanted to move and instead fully allowed Him to move the way He wanted, we began to see tremendous breakthroughs.

At first it was difficult to let go of our control. Although we did not view ourselves as controlling, we were. This is because we feared losing control, as if people would get weird and flaky. But even more than that, we feared doing something wrong. My husband and I never would have wanted to lead the congregation in a wrong direction. We wanted to provide a place of "safety" and "refuge." Opening our services to something "new" meant we had to become more vulnerable, and we felt a sincere responsibility to protect the sheep over whom God had given us charge.

Yet when we backed off and trusted the Holy Spirit to direct us through each service, it was always powerful! We had tapped into a River of anointing that we had never experienced before. We witnessed signs and wonders, healings and a new level of prophetic ministry. At times we were unable to preach, so we simply ministered in healing, prophecy and deliverance as directed by His Spirit. Sometimes we could not walk to the pulpit but fell flat on our faces. But He was always in control, and as a result no one got weird or strange, or tried to take over the service.

In my flesh I felt totally out of control. My spirit, however, was abounding. Every time I would attempt to take back control, I would quench the anointing. I learned to trust Him, to back away from my mind-sets and allow His Holy Spirit to move and minister. There was always proper order—submission to authority—as we maintained a reverence for the Holy Spirit. If I were to label this as receiving from one of God's sevenfold attributes, I would say that we were embracing the fear of the Lord. We became so fearful of grieving the Holy Spirit that we always preferred His way over our own way.

Even the Patriarchs Had Paradigms

When a person has a religious paradigm, a mind-set or limited thinking, it is quite obvious. It is revealed in his or her responses to God's word. If God says a person can be healed, for example, the person with a religious mind-set might respond, "But the doctor said I only have a few months to live!" Or if a person receives a prophecy that declares, "You are going to buy a new car," his or her paradigm will say, "But I can't even pay my rent!"

Even the biblical patriarchs had paradigms. We already discussed Zacharias. Abraham presents another example of limited thinking. In a vision God told him, "Your reward will be great!" Abraham's mind-set spoke, "But I am childless" (see Genesis 15:1–2). Sarah had the same mind-set; they both laughed at the prophecies.

And what about Gideon? From the very beginning, we notice Gideon's paradigm—his mind-sets—concerning the Lord. An angel appeared and said to him, "God is with you!" Gideon's paradigm immediately spoke concerning God's ability to protect him and the Israelites and said, "How can God be with us? And by the way, where are the miracles?" His response concerning his beliefs about

God came from the extreme oppression he and his nation had experienced from their enemies, the Midianites (see Judges 6:13).

Gideon also hid his grain from the Midianites. Hiding his provision represented a fear that the enemy would steal from him. Many of us do the same thing with our finances; we hoard our money out of a fear of lack. Gideon obviously had a poverty mentality and could not trust God for his safety and provision.

The Church today seems to be confronted with the same paradigm beliefs as Gideon. In many of our present situations, we may have suffered lack, sickness, oppression and hopelessness, and our paradigms speak those instead of faith in God's power.

What if a person is struggling with some life difficulty, and then goes to a church meeting where he is given a prophetic word that says, "Rejoice! God is with you!"? Most likely the person's religious paradigm will immediately speak the opposite: "But how can He be with me when I am going through what I am going through?" Just like the biblical patriarchs—and matriarchs, too—we struggle with old belief systems. In order to break free from old, established paradigms that hinder our faith, we must shift into a new belief system. We must begin to believe the Word of God and trust in the God of our breakthrough.

Paradigms about Ourselves

Gideon did not just have a false belief system concerning God; his paradigms concerning himself also were exposed. God called to him, "Gideon, mighty man of valor!" Gideon's belief system—his paradigms that limited his thinking—spoke immediately and said, "I am the very least among my people!" (see Judges 6:15).

Many of us respond the same as Gideon. When God speaks into our destiny, our response is, "Who, me? But God, don't You know I don't speak so well? I'm not old enough. I haven't been to seminary, and I didn't do well in school."

Some of my paradigms have sounded like:

"God, I don't have time to take on more responsibility."
"God, I don't have the energy to do what You are requiring."
"God, I am not certain I am able to pastor a church."
"God, I can't speak well."
"God, how can I deal with one more challenge?"
"God, You want me to do *what*?!"
"Who, *me*?"

It has taken quite a while to get to the victory side of some of these paradigms, and I am still working on accomplishing victory over the others. But looking back, I am so grateful God overlooked my doubt and unbelief. He kept speaking into my untapped potential until I finally aligned myself with the truth of what He spoke.

There will be a season when God will confront your paradigms. You will be challenged with all that God sees in you. He will speak to your potential and then expect you to shift out of any old paradigms that limit you from fulfilling your destiny.

Tear Down Your Idols

Gideon's primary assignment was to destroy the idols that were in his own backyard. Before he was fully empowered to lead the Israelites into battle, he had to first destroy the idols of his ancestors.

We have to remember how much God hates idolatry. Worshiping idols is not limited to bowing down to a statue of Buddha or a tangible graven image. If we exalt the enemy's words above God's words, then we are committing idolatry. God and His Word are one, and they cannot be separated from each other. If we place Satan's words about us—words such as *useless, unable to succeed, hopeless, failure, rejected, abandoned* and *shameful*—above what God has said—that we are the head and not the tail, blessed, healed, delivered, successful, anointed, loved and accepted—then we are committing idolatry! If we believe the lies of the devil, then it is time to relandscape our backyards, as Gideon did. As we tear down false belief systems, we also are tearing down old structures that have been domineering paradigms of thinking.

As I stated before, paradigms resist change. But in order to move forward, God requires that we make paradigm shifts. This means renewing our minds by tearing down false idols and fully accepting God's Word concerning us.

Tearing down paradigms and reestablishing God's truth is a spiritual battle. But, oh, is it worth the time and effort when we move into that new and awesome place of victory!

Three Requirements for a New Paradigm

Are you now ready to shift and transition into a new level of His glory? Are you excited about heaven touching earth?

Three things are required in order to make this giant leap into God's new thing:

1. Allow God to intervene at any time He desires.
2. Allow God to change your vision.
3. Allow God to continually expand your vision and empower you to move from glory to greater levels of glory.

First, we must always allow God to intervene in our thoughts and our actions—especially within our ministry times. As a former pastor, I really believed I did this until the Lord challenged me with an old paradigm. It was not that I had a problem with a move of His Spirit; the problem was with the persecution that occurred as a result of His moving! Many people say they want God to move freely, yet when He does, their religious mind-sets are challenged. God is releasing His River, and we must not limit flowing in this River. God will do a new thing with a release of His flood. We must hear by the Spirit as to how He desires to minister and not limit Him because of how He used to minister.

When persecution comes because you have allowed the Holy Spirit the freedom to minister, you will be tempted to stop. Do not stop, and do not look back. The solution to persecution is not to run but to embrace the fireball. Become addicted to radical passion, and you will make it across to the other side of your test.

Second, allow God to expand your vision. A vision can become a paradigm within itself. Think about this for a moment. We often believe that we must maintain the original vision. We make the vision plain. We print the vision in the bulletins and discuss it with others in the congregation. It becomes the vision of the church and ministry, and everyone who colabors with us catches the vision.

A vision, however, is not etched in stone like the Ten Commandments! And even the Ten Commandments were somewhat revised when Jesus introduced His Kingdom message. So most likely our vision will change as the Holy Spirit intervenes.

If we have a religious paradigm, then we might have trouble with this one requirement. And if we have not fulfilled the first vision, we will especially tend to hang onto the old way to ensure that it is fulfilled.

We must ask ourselves this question: *Did God really give us that original vision, or was it partly our own desires?* You see, most of the time our own personal desires are expressed in a vision, and then later the Lord purifies it. As a result, it all becomes His vision, and we are simply following the leading of His Spirit when He changes and sanctifies it. Remember this one statement: *It is not about us; it is all about Him!*

Third, when He expands the vision, allow Him to keep expanding! Don't lock into another paradigm after the first major shift. Keep moving and shifting. The Scripture says that we move from faith to faith, strength to strength and glory to glory: "But we all, with unveiled face, beholding as in a mirror the glory of the Lord, are being transformed into the same image from glory to glory, just as by the Spirit of the Lord" (2 Corinthians 3:18, NKJV). This means that He will challenge us with new levels of faith and give us strength for every new level, which will empower us to embrace glory, more glory and even greater levels of His glory.

Let's commit now to move from our old paradigms, embrace God's new thing for us and move from glory to glory!

Points to Consider

1. God speaks differently during transition. Be careful not to limit His direction based on how He spoke in the past.
2. In times of transition, it is more beneficial to embrace a new level of faith rather than to speak quickly against new direction. Remember, God had to shut the mouth of Zacharias so that the Word of the Lord would be fulfilled.
3. Be on guard and protect each infilling of His power. Remember, the children of Israel got filled up with great faith, but by the third day, they began to leak.

4. A paradigm is a mental structure that limits us. Don't allow any structure that opposes God's "new thing" to remain in position.
5. If you are feeling pressure from the paradigm shift, you are in good company. The patriarchs of old are in your winner's circle!
6. Radical behavior is required during these radical seasons of change.
7. It is not about us; it is all about Him!

5

THE NEW THING

"Forget the former things; do not dwell on the past. See, I am doing a new thing! Now it springs up; do you not perceive it? I am making a way in the desert and streams in the wasteland."

Isaiah 43:18–19

What is a "new thing"? Something new represents an item never possessed before, whether it is a material item or something spiritual, such as revelation, gifting, etc. It might also represent a place never visited, an action not yet taken or a thought never before formed.

When I purchase a new car, it is new to me, but it may have been on the car dealer's sales lot for a year. When I receive it, it is my "new car." Similarly, when God says He is going to do a new thing, it does not necessarily mean He is planning to do something today that was not available yesterday. He is "the same yesterday and today and forever" (Hebrews 13:8). The divine revelation we are receiving today has always been available; He has just been waiting for us to grab hold of fresh revelation and run with it!

We need to recognize that He is doing a new thing, and in fact, it has already begun. "And afterward, I will pour out my Spirit on all people. Your sons and daughters will prophesy, your old men will dream dreams, your young men will see visions" (Joel 2:28). He *is* pouring out His Spirit upon all flesh, and we are witnessing a divine fulfillment of Joel 2:28 with a dynamic release of the supernatural.

The requirements for embracing this new thing are mentioned in Isaiah 43:18–19: "Forget the former things; do not dwell on the past. See, I am doing a new thing! Now it springs up; do you not perceive it? I am making a way in the desert and streams in the wasteland." This Scripture tells us three things we must do to embrace this new thing:

1. As God does a new thing, we must know it.
2. We must come out of the wilderness.
3. We must jump in the river that leads us out of the wilderness and our desert.

Your Wilderness Involves a "Coming Out" Process

Song of Solomon 3:6 symbolizes the bride who is coming out of the wilderness: "Who is this coming up from the desert like a column of smoke, perfumed with myrrh and incense made from all the spices of the merchant?" The bride has been prepared with the fragrance of myrrh and has been groomed for intimacy with the bridegroom. This dynamic and illustrative passage is symbolic of the process of shifting from a past wilderness lifestyle into a covenant relationship with Christ.

I remember the day I was going to marry my husband, Mickey. Although he is a wonderful, God-fearing man, I began to struggle with a fear of the unknown. What would my future hold? What would marriage be like? Would I be a good wife? All of these questions began to trouble me as I was coming out of my "wilderness of singleness." Maybe this is where the "runaway bride syndrome" comes from.

Spiritually, it is the same scenario for each of us when we come into covenant with God. As the Bridegroom beckons us to the altar of commitment and change—leading us into the "new thing"—we, as the Bride of Christ, must be fully committed to "come out" of the wilderness lifestyle. We must begin to shift out of old mind-sets concerning our future. We must begin to let go of the past and embrace a new future by embracing His "new thing."

Our wilderness experience is over when we allow ourselves to meet and experience covenant with the Bridegroom. Old religious paradigms fall to the wayside as we walk a new path with our covenant partner, Christ Jesus. He becomes our Husband and leads us into all truth.

We all are aware that shifting out of familiar territory into an unknown future is frightening, but on the other hand, remaining in an old religious structure limits us. Although we might be tempted to run away from the challenge of the new covenant relationship, we must decide to draw even closer in order to hear His voice and experience change.

We cannot be "fruitful and multiply" without marriage. In the spiritual realm, we are limited and, therefore, unfruitful if we remain in a rigid religious structure.

Understanding Religious Culture

When I graduated from college, I received a degree that prepared me to teach four different subjects. One of them was sociology, the study of society, its origin and fundamental laws. I have always been fascinated with people—how they form communities, what frames their belief systems and what behavioral patterns dictate their mores and culture.

Most of us have a certain culture in our communities, homes, businesses, churches and ministries. A culture is what is "cultivated" in our lives. As we cultivate a belief system over and over on a daily basis, it gains a stronghold. A stronghold is like a castle or a prison that literally imprisons us to our past. The stronghold is so much a part of us that it becomes a culture.

When I became a teacher of God's Word, I realized there is a "religious culture"—an established form of beliefs that is reinforced daily and that is determined by particular styles of worship, preaching and interpretations of the Bible. The Church holds established belief systems that shape and mold its religious communities. Many belief systems, however, have become religious paradigms. And any reinforced belief system can result in religious "tradition," which can easily become a stronghold—and then the stronghold becomes a "religious culture." We then respond to God and His Spirit out of that religious culture.

To put these spiritual dynamics in simple terms, I would challenge you to examine your environment. If you were to carefully observe your home, what would you say was cultivated on a daily basis? Does your home environment cultivate faith and a positive mental attitude? Does your spiritual head promote spiritual authority, respect for elders and strong morals? What is cultivated becomes your home's established culture.

What is the culture of your church? Do you cultivate an atmosphere that embraces the fullness of the Holy Spirit? Do you allow time for worship, prophetic ministry, healing and sound teaching? Whatever is cultivated in your church becomes your church culture.

Unfortunately, far too many of us have cultivated the wrong crops. Our culture is based on negativity, limited paradigms, old patterns of behavior, doubt, unbelief, limiting mind-sets and old religious structures. With these dynamics in our culture, how in the world can we embrace God's new thing? The only way is to come out of that dry, desolate place and jump into the River of Life! We must come out of our old religious culture in order to influence the spiritual atmosphere and experience God's new thing.

The Pharisees Had a Culture

Old belief systems prevent God's new thing. The Pharisees are perhaps the best biblical example of this mistake. The Pharisees were holy on the outside, but they never understood God's love. They studied the Law. They cultivated long, endless, lifeless prayers. They had rules, regulations and expectations that were part of the old system, based on the Law of Moses. Their belief system became their culture, and when the new came, they would not shift out of it.

The Pharisees were set in their ways. Even Jesus could not break their religious traditions and reveal new truths. He had to raise up twelve others who were not entrenched in religiosity to teach the Pharisees the pure message of the Kingdom of God.

Jesus did not come to bring peace to their religious system. He came to shake their world. He upset their religious system—just as He is upsetting ours today.

Like the Pharisees in Jesus' time, many today are not willing to shift because they truly believe the old is better. God, however, is pouring out a new wine. And He is pouring it out now!

New Wine Requires New Wineskins

"And no one puts new wine into old wineskins. For the new wine would burst the wineskins, spilling the wine and ruining the skins. New wine must be stored in new wineskins. But no one who drinks the old wine seems to want the new wine. 'The old is just fine,' they say."

Luke 5:37–39, NLT

Some of the wineskins are unprepared, and it is causing a lot of ripping and tearing. Don't think God will wait until everyone is ready. He is not limited to our being ready for Him. He is in charge, and He is allowing some ripping and tearing so that we can see what parts of our lives are unprepared for the fullness of His Spirit.

Many of us feel that ripping and tearing is a terrible atrocity. And to a degree, it is. But that ripping, tearing and trouble is certainly getting our attention as to what needs to be fixed in order to prepare for His new thing! And God is allowing it. You are wasting time if you are binding the devil when it is God in the midst of the shaking.

Ask yourself what part of your belief system is unable to handle this fresh move of His Spirit. What is it that bothers you when God changes the order of the church service? Are you so set on a certain "order" or "structure" that there is no room for the Holy Spirit?

When my husband and I were pastoring a local church, we just knew that God would move after we sang three fast songs and three slow songs. That was our strategy to prepare the way for God's Spirit to minister to the congregation. We always began with a fast song. Then one day the Lord spoke to me and said, *Okay, will you let Me decide what songs to sing?* At first, it really shook me. I thought we had been allowing Him to lead. Once we decided that there would no longer be a "formula" to follow, we were able to fully shift into a new place.

I am not saying that we never need a plan. We still discuss every service with our worship leader. All of us, however, are ready to shift at any time into a different song or direction at the leading of the Holy Spirit. By fully submitting to His divine direction, we have experienced more anointing and breakthrough than ever before.

We did not come into that new place of breakthrough easily or overnight. It took a lot of ripping and tearing. We have been in ministry for over seventeen years, and we just now feel that we have gained some understanding on how to follow His Spirit.

But just about the time we have it figured out, He changes on us! I am positive this is because He desires that we remain flexible in order to move in any direction. He requires that we remain new wineskins, always able to hold the new wine He pours into us.

Changing the Spiritual Atmosphere

Embracing a new thing requires changing our spiritual atmosphere. In order to do this, we often need a fresh start. We must renew our wineskins.

When I realized it was time for a fresh start, I decided to go back to the book of Genesis to discover who I really was. I once again realized that God created me in His image and that He gave me power and dominion on this earth. I began to read more materials on dominion and authority, and before I knew it, I was walking in authority. Suddenly I realized I was talking differently, praying differently and, as my husband says, "Hallelujah, acting differently!" Then, I noticed my environment beginning to change. Others around me were becoming more positive, and they also began to take authority. This is an example of changing your atmosphere.

When you decide to shift out of the old, first realize that you are already seated in heavenly places. To experience a spiritual shift, we must begin to take godly authority over the atmosphere. By using spiritual discernment, we can bind negative spirits in operation, take authority over spirits of darkness and, if necessary, cast out devils. We should not back away from this challenge, because it is the only way that we can spiritually shift the atmosphere.

Negative Climates Block the New Thing

God's new thing can be blocked by a negative climate. Remember when the spies went into Canaan? They entered into an atmosphere of demonic oppression. They became influenced by the territorial strongholds of doubt and unbelief. They took this spiritual climate back into the camp of Israel, and this negativity "rubbed off" on the entire nation. The spies' doubt and unbelief became an established culture, which was cultivated for years to come. In fact, it became so much a part of them that God had to allow the entire generation to die in the wilderness in order to kill the "old culture." Only Joshua and Caleb, the only ones with a positive report, were empowered to cross over into their destinies.

It is the same for us today. We must maintain a positive approach whenever God is requiring us to embrace a new thing. We cannot allow old patterns of behavior to rob us of our promise. We must prepare our hearts to cross over into our Promised Land. If our faith is in religious structure, we will miss our breakthrough into our places of promise. It is time to shift out of religious paradigms, limited thinking and tradition to fully embrace His glory.

Don't Trust Your Emotions

To embrace God's new thing, we must remain focused on God's Word and His Spirit—not our emotions. Because our mind-sets become strongholds that limit us, we can never fully trust our emotions. Nor can we trust old belief systems and old structures. As I said, old belief systems become strongholds that bind us to our past and keep us from embracing the fullness of His Spirit.

Our emotions get in the way. When Jesus asked Peter, "Who do you say I am?" Peter responded with great zeal and divine revelation and said, "You are the Christ, the Son of the living God" (see Matthew 16:15–19). Jesus was so impressed with Peter's answer that He said He was going to build His entire Church upon that revelation. But later when Jesus announced that He would die, Peter moved out of that place of tremendous revelation and said, "Not so!" Jesus turned to rebuke him, saying, "Get behind me, Satan!" (Matthew 16:23).

During times of change, we must not trust ourselves. We must remember to remain focused on God's Word and His Spirit, or else our emotions will win over. By constantly cultivating a new religious culture, we can reinforce our thinking processes to fully embrace truth.

Overthrowing Death Structures

Embracing God's new thing involves overthrowing death structures. Although I discuss this in greater detail in chapter 12, I will disclose here a measure of understanding regarding the effects of a death structure.

Whatever is not releasing life must be recognized as possibly releasing death, and so we call these "death structures." *Webster's Dictionary* defines *structure* as "the manner of which something is constructed, as a building or a bridge. It implies how something is built."[1] It actually refers to the construction of the body parts and organs. A structure is similar to a framework in its definition. When considering our bodies, we often refer to our "body frame," which involves body structure and its bones. Bones provide structural support for all the organs. In a spiritual sense, a structure is the framework of any organization, belief system or doctrine.

The Scripture states that wherever there is legalism, there is death: "He has made us competent as ministers of a new covenant—not of the letter but of the Spirit; for the letter kills, but the Spirit gives life" (2 Corinthians 3:6).

It is clear that if we are led by the law, doctrines or a religious system and not by the Holy Spirit, then we experience death rather than life. It is sad how many "dead" churches there are because they have not given the Spirit of God the opportunity to minister life.

The Body of Christ is in a season of overthrowing death structures. God has a new framework planned that will release resurrection power to the Body of Christ. We need God's resurrection power to flow so that He can resurrect dead churches. God is going to restructure His Church so that we can have the mantle of Elisha.

Elisha's Mantle

Elisha performed twice the number of miracles that his mentor, Elijah, did. He is well-known for following Elijah all the way to the end. He was faithful to serve Elijah even when Elijah tried to leave him behind! He was at the Jordan when the Lord took Elijah to heaven, and then he took Elijah's mantle and divided the Jordan River with it.

He purified water, pronounced curses with results, foretold successes and supernaturally provided for widows. He raised the dead, took poison out of food and fed the one hundred with little substance. He healed Naaman of leprosy, made an axe head float and exposed the secret battle plans of Syria to the king. He prayed for his servant to see the supernatural, blinded an entire army and foretold deaths and victories. Even after his death, when a dead man's body was thrown into the grave with Elisha's bones, the dead man was resurrected! Wow!

The bones—the structure—of Elisha is what the Church needs today. We need a structure of life-giving resurrection power to flow in our churches, ministries and lives. In order to have this type of power, we must make a spiritual shift and embrace the miraculous, move in miracles and allow the Holy Spirit to move in power and might. In order to embrace God's new thing, we must take up the mantle of Elisha.

"Them Bones, Them Bones, Them Dry Bones"

In Ezekiel 37, the prophet was to prophesy to an army of dry bones lying in a valley. This army was dead. He was being called to speak prophetically to an old, dead, dry structure.

As a prophetic revelation for today, I believe that the dead army represents all the dead religion to which God desires to speak life. Picture this: The Elijah Company, a group of today's anointed prophets, approaches these dead bones—dead church structures with no life in them. As He asked Ezekiel, God asks the prophets, "Can these dead structures live?" Looking in the natural, the prophets respond, "O God, only You would know. Actually, to us it seems impossible!" Then the Lord, because He is a God of hope, life and breakthrough, instructs the prophets to speak to the old, dry, dead religious structures, just as He told Ezekiel to speak to those dead bones in the valley: "Tell these dead religious structures to become alive! Tell these dead structures to come together and form a brand-new living, breathing mechanism that will embrace My breath and move by My Spirit!"

Dear ones, God is calling us to speak to the dead bones. He is calling us to speak His life to our churches, so that His new thing can overflow in them.

Unclean Spirits Will Cry "Leave Us Alone!"

When Jesus cast out the unclean spirits, they cried out and told Him to leave them alone, to not cast them out (see Mark 1:24). Unclean religious spirits always make noise when they have to let go of old structures.

These demonic spirits rise up and say, "Leave us alone! Leave the Church the way it is. We like the old structure. We don't want to change!"

When God begins to change our structure, we will hear that noise. And if we truly are embracing the new thing, we will not listen to the voices of these demonic spirits. We will arise from our shrouds of death and embrace the newness of life. Our structure will come together, and we will form a great and mighty army. Hallelujah!

Are You Ready to Embrace God's New Thing?

Are you ready to receive a fresh breath of life? Have you felt dead and dry, and you know it is because you have decided it is impossible to change? Well, precious ones, all that is needed is to repent and be determined to change. Rise up and embrace life today!

Now in order to shift out from your wilderness, you need to take immediate action:

- List below the issues in your life that keep you in your wilderness.

- Now list how you desire God to use you as you decide to come out of your wilderness.

  — Be a blessing to all I come in contact w.

- List the Scriptures that will empower you as you step out of your wilderness.

- Now speak the Scriptures aloud so that the devil hears the Word of God. Command the devil to flee because God already has your destiny planned.

- Describe the new structure that you desire for your life, and thank God that He will empower you to make the shift into the "new thing."

- Now, are you ready? Shift! And don't look back!

6

8/7/08

HE IS BACK FROM THE FUTURE

Let them praise the name of the LORD, for his name alone is
exalted; his splendor is above the earth and the heavens.

Psalm 148:13

Unlike us, who are known by only a few names and possibly nicknames, God has many different names. When
Scripture refers to a *name of God*, the Hebrew word *shem*
is used, which implies what someone is famous for.[1] Isn't
that an awesome thought? The names of God tell us what
He is famous, or known, for. All the names of God are the
attributes of what He has done and is still able to do for us.
The names of God imply His reputation, His glory (what
He receives glory for being and doing) and His fame.

The word *name* is also derived from another Hebrew
word, *suwm*, which implies that through a name an establishment occurs.[2] In other words, God's names bring divine

order. Through God's many different names, He sets our circumstances into divine order by releasing the attributes each name implies.

Throughout Scripture, the Lord revealed Himself through many different names. The first was *Elohim*, the "Creator God," "the Three in One" (see Genesis 1:1). It was *El Elyon*, "God Most High," who delivered Abraham's enemies into his hand (see Genesis 14:20). Genesis 22 tells how God tested Abraham, and after the test Abraham called Him *Jehovah Jireh*, because He is the "God who provides." Each time God desired to reveal an attribute of His fame, reputation and glory, He would reveal a new name. By revealing His name, He would set things in divine order so that the attributes of His name could be accomplished.

When He made Himself known as *Jehovah Rapha*, "God our Healer," He revealed that He is the God who heals us. *Jehovah Shalom* means He is the "God of peace." As He reveals these two names to us today, He establishes healing and peace in our lives. When we are struggling with finances, we know that He is *Jehovah Jireh*, "God our Provider," and that He can supply all our needs. Our only responsibility is to receive that attribute with faith in His name and believe that He is able to provide.

Understanding that He is able to establish all that His names declare is an awesome revelation. Knowing His names and that He desires to bless us with His attributes empowers us to move forward and fulfill our divine destiny.

Up until the time Moses approached Pharaoh, both Moses and the Israelites were trusting God by only one name. They related to God as *El Shaddai* and did not fully understand Him by any other name.

The name *El Shaddai* can be translated as "the many-breasted one" and represents the mothering nature of God. The name reminds us of a mother bear who viciously fights any predator that intends to harm her young. In *El Shaddai*, we recognize the warrior nature of God rising up as a mothering protector. Up until then, Israel had witnessed only this aspect of God's character, since He had revealed Himself as the One who "mothered" the Israelites—fed, nurtured and protected them.

Not until they were released from Egyptian captivity did God fully challenge them to embrace the different attributes of His name. The Lord was maturing His children and He had other attributes of His character that He desired them to understand and embrace.

In Exodus 6, God instructed Moses to approach Pharaoh and demand that he "Let God's people go!" Moses resisted God's instructions. He argued with God and reminded Him that the children of Israel would not listen to him. Then God told Moses that He was *Jehovah* ("Lord") and that the past generations had only understood Him as "God Almighty."

> And God spake unto Moses, and said unto him, I am the Lord: and I appeared unto Abraham, unto Isaac, and unto Jacob, by the name of God Almighty, but by my name Jehovah was I not known to them. And I have also established my covenant with them, to give them the land of Canaan, the land of their pilgrimage, wherein they were strangers.
>
> Exodus 6:2–4, KJV

God as *Jehovah* was revealing Himself to His people. This was very exciting because the name *Jehovah* represents the God of our future! It means "the all-existing One," "God who is and was and is evermore to be." The Israelites had never fully embraced Him as Lord. But God wanted them to understand this aspect of His nature. And furthermore, God as Lord told Moses that through that name He had established covenant with His people and would deliver them.

It was time for the Israelites to be released from their season of bondage into their future of crossing over into their place of promise. God was revealing Himself as the God of their future. He is the One who was in the beginning and knows the end. Therefore, He is the God who is back from the future!

He Is the God of Our Future

We can know God by His many different names. But how comforting this name, Jehovah, is! Jehovah, the LORD, is the God who knows our future and is releasing us to our future.

Saints, because it is our season to shift out of the old and into the new, we must make a giant leap out of our old mind-sets that limit our view of God. Remember: He is LORD! He knows our future and is able to accomplish what He has promised.

> "'Behold, the days are coming,' says the LORD, 'that I will perform that good thing which I have promised to the house of Israel and to the house of Judah.'"
>
> Jeremiah 33:14, NKJV

If we were totally honest with ourselves, we would admit that we, like the Israelites before their release from captivity, have limited God and His ability to accomplish what He has promised. We have doubted that He desires to bring the plans of heaven to this earth. Our doubt and unbelief have become strongholds that have limited our faith to receive God's best for our lives. This is the reason why we must shift out of our mind-sets and religious paradigms.

Limiting God to the Past

In addition to limiting God's ability, the Israelites limited Him to how He spoke in the past. When they were in Egypt, they were in bondage to Pharaoh. For over four hundred years they had cried out for a deliverer. Every day was consumed with praying for a deliverer. And when they were finally delivered, they were tested in the wilderness and began to cry out for another deliverer! Because God had answered them by sending them a deliverer in the past, they expected to be delivered out of their circumstances again. At the time of their very first testing at the bitter waters, they cried out to be delivered from their situation rather than believing God to provide.

We, too, limit God to how He spoke in the past. I have seen businessmen, for example, expect God to move the same way He did over a decade ago. They trusted old patterns of employment opportunities, investments and economic forecasts. When God began to bring change, they suffered loss and confusion. If we are not careful, we will do the same.

In this new season, God is challenging us to believe for a breakthrough, to believe for the manifestation of His glory in the situation rather than for a simple deliverance out of the situation. We can no longer trust old patterns. We must develop spiritual ears to hear new direction given by the Holy Spirit.

Even Moses related to God from an old pattern. In Numbers 20, Israel was in the wilderness, and once again the congregation was thirsty. The usual pattern for the Israelites was to blame Moses and Aaron for their problems, and this time was no exception. This time the Lord instructed Moses to speak to the rock, and as a result water would gush forth. It was a different strategy than before, when Moses had been told to strike the rock.

In disobedience, Moses struck the rock rather than speaking to it. Now we know that the people of Israel had provoked Moses beyond measure, but that is not a good enough excuse to disobey willfully the voice of the Lord. But it is also possible that Moses had an old mind-set and was having trouble shifting from a previous paradigm into present-day instruction. Moses had known God's voice as He spoke to him in the past. Now God was changing His breakthrough strategy for Moses. Moses might have thought, *Surely that wasn't God's voice! The last time He said to strike the rock. Maybe I misunderstood Him this time.* Acting out of an old paradigm caused Moses to be disobedient, and his lack of total submission cost him his future in the Promised Land.

Oh my goodness, we do not want to miss our promise, do we? Then we had better make quick shifts out from old paradigms because they limit our reception of the voice of the Lord.

Shifting into a New Place with God

The Israelites could not shift. In fact, Moses himself could not totally shift. In Exodus 6:7–8, God told Moses He would bring the Israelites out from under the yoke of the Egyptians. But Israel could not shift out of her paradigm of an old slavery mentality. The people were enslaved to a structure that limited their faith, and, therefore, they continued to see themselves as slaves.

Even Moses could not see himself as God saw him. He continued to remind God of his speech impediment and made excuses based on his perceived inadequacies. However, God reminded Moses that He had made him a god to Pharaoh.

Do you realize that when the devil looks at you, he sees Jesus? If you are born again, then you are Christ-like. And like Moses, when you approach the Pharaoh in your life, you can demand that the enemy loose you from bondage and let you go—for you are like a god to your Pharaoh.

This, saints of the Most High, is how you begin to shift into your new place with God. By realizing who you are in Christ Jesus, you become supernaturally empowered to face your enemy, confront your enemy and be released into your future!

I have been challenged with the very same concerns as most of you who are reading this book. Whenever God begins to speak new things to us, we are immediately challenged with our old paradigms. I can remember when Spirit-led laughter came into our church. The release of joy and laughter was wonderful and refreshing, but I still struggled with mind-sets concerning this new wine. I knew this was a divine move of God's Spirit, but I remember feeling out of control and being concerned about how others might view God's new move. Unfortunately, this "new thing" of God was misunderstood and labeled as flaky. Some of our congregation actually left the church because the way God was moving did not fit into their religious paradigms. It would have been easier to embrace a new move of the Holy Spirit if I had not had to contend with the religious spirits that came immediately to discredit us and our integrity.

Many moves of the Holy Spirit have been misunderstood and improperly judged, mainly because of religious paradigms and mind-sets. This is very unfortunate, because God wants to bless us and pour out the fullness of His Spirit. Unless we trust Him, we will never make the full shift into the fullness of His Kingdom message where heaven actually comes to earth.

The Vision of His Fireball

I remember another time I was challenged with old paradigms. After my husband and I stopped pastoring a local church and embraced our new responsibilities as traveling ministers, God began to speak to us concerning a Kingdom Training Center. Suddenly we were being challenged with something different—a training center that we would apostolically oversee. We were no longer pastors; we were transitioning into becoming apostles. Although this was clearly a new assignment and a different concept of training, I knew it was God who was speaking to us concerning this new venture. At first my paradigms, which limited my ability, arose: *God, what do You mean, build a Kingdom Training Center? What is a Kingdom Training Center? God, we cannot do that!*

Then I had a vision that helped me shift into God's new thing for us. I clearly saw a fireball hurtling toward me. I instantly knew the fireball was from heaven. It was sent by His words over me. As it came closer, the Lord said, *Keep what I have just spoken holy.* He went on, *Separate what I have just spoken and keep it holy before Me. Do not allow it to become defiled with doubt and unbelief, but place it firmly in your heart. Do not allow the enemy to steal it from you, but keep it holy before Me.*

I knew God was very serious about what He had just spoken. With fear and trembling, I jumped up and ran to find pen and paper to write down the vision. Within a few minutes, I found myself in the Scriptures studying Moses' encounter with the very same instructions.

Keeping It Holy

Moses dealt with the same encounter as I did! When Moses met God, the first thing God said was for Moses to take off his shoes, for the ground on which he was standing was holy. Actually, not one molecule in that ground had changed, but because God said it was holy, it became holy ground. But it was more than simply the dirt that was holy; God was also addressing the ground of Moses' heart. What

God was speaking into Moses' heart was holy, and Moses was instructed to separate it from what he thought about himself, to realize his potential and to embrace the holiness of God's will over his life. What God was about to declare over Moses was holy, and every time Moses doubted his call, he was to separate it from his head knowledge and keep holy what God had said.

When we are shifting into our Promised Land, the thief attempts to steal our destiny. We must guard against the thief.[3] How? We must be like Moses at the burning bush. To everything God speaks to us, we must respond as if we were standing in front of the burning bush. We must treat the ground as "holy." Even if we feel inadequate, we must believe that we are well able to take our land.

Can you imagine how worn out Moses was toward the end of his wilderness journey? I suppose he had to constantly protect his heart every time he was challenged in the desert place. "Keeping it holy" through the dry seasons is difficult, especially when the devil is tempting you to quit the race and throw in the towel. When the Israelites needed another drink of water, their murmuring provoked Moses to strike the rock. He failed to keep God's instructions to speak to the rock as "holy and separated" from his emotions. This act of disobedience cancelled his crossing over into his promise.

No matter how difficult it may be, separate yourself from your emotions during the season of transition. Emotions are connected to past circumstances, frustrations and fears. Separate yourself unto the Lord and allow Him to empower you to shift into your place of enlargement.

Leap into Your Future!

It is not easy to leave home, especially when we have been close to our parents. My parents had to kick me out of the nest because I had become dependent on their protection, their insight and their money!

Even as a college student, I enjoyed the carefree dormitory lifestyle where my tuition and housing were provided by my parents. I remember one summer I decided to pursue summer employment. I moved into an apartment and found a job. Being a student does not impress an employer and it does not warrant large salaries, so I received minimum wage. Needless to say, it was a hungry summer! I lasted three months in the workforce and then went back to college for the easy life. I knew when I had a good thing going on!

When it came time to leave home permanently, I was terribly afraid. Although I was getting married, insecurity regarding my future tormented me. *What if we don't have enough money? What if I have to go to work and can't find a decent job?* These thoughts troubled me for days before our wedding. Finally my mother sat me down and said, "Sandie, you have to leave now!"

Looking back, I realize that I was dependent on my parents' "mothering nature." I felt comfort, security and peace when I was home.

When it is time for us to step out and leave "home"—our secure place—we have to let go of our *El Shaddai* and begin to embrace the LORD (*Jehovah*), the God of our future. God will still be our comforter and protector, as a mother who watches over her children, but there comes a time when we have to be pushed out of our nest. Otherwise, we will never grow up and move forward.

A mother eagle prepares her eaglets to leave their nest by removing pieces of soft down a little at a time. Over a period of a few days the soft down is removed and all that is left is a nest full of sharp twigs and thorns. The eaglets have no choice but to leave that old, sticky nest and fly away.

It is the same with each of us when God prepares us to take a leap of faith and shift out of an old place. He begins to make our lives uncomfortable. We become dissatisfied; we are dry and thirsty and realize we need change. God has caused our place of comfort to become very uncomfortable, and we have no choice but to leave our old nest. This is when the LORD, *Jehovah*, the God of our future, takes over.

Our role is to use the heavenly strategies He has given us:

1. Remember that God does not sound the same when you are in transition.
2. Remember to keep what God says to you "holy" during this time of transition.
3. Remember that the God of your future desires to reveal Himself to you.

Trust His Word. Listen to His new voice. Keep what He says holy. And meet Him in a new way.

I encourage you to leap into your future. The God of your future awaits your arrival!

Thoughts to Consider

- Has the Lord spoken something "different" to you? In other words, are you right in the middle of a "shift"? Then most likely you are going to be required to "keep it holy." List below how you will set His plan aside and "keep it holy."

- Is God revealing Himself to you as the God of your future? What prophetic words have you received that involve shifting into the new? List below your plans for the future and how you are determined to make the shift.

• Name the "fireball" that you must embrace as you shift into your future. Then write a prayer to the Lord asking for His divine grace as you embrace His fireball.

7

Coming Out of the Wilderness

So Moses brought Israel from the Red Sea; then they went out into the *Wilderness* of Shur. And they went three days in the *wilderness* and found no water.

Exodus 15:22, NKJV, emphasis mine

Most of us use every ounce of faith and energy attempting to leave a place called "Here" to get to that Promised Land of "There." As we travel to "There," a season of transition and change is required. Transition, simply stated, is moving from one place to another.

This implies that in order to fully arrive "There," we must be willing to let go of the old nature. Our destiny and fulfillment in God requires us to shift out of an old place and enter into the new.

While moving toward the "There," many of us have experienced a wilderness. According to *Webster's Dictionary*, the word *wilderness* is described as:

1. a desert (sandy-filled area),
2. an uncultivated and uninhabited territory, wild; living in the "wild,"
3. a state of disorder.[1]

The book of Exodus documents the "wilderness" as the region where the children of Israel wandered for forty years. Their wilderness consisted of many tests and challenges as God measured their faith and obedience. It is interesting to note that the word *wilderness* in Hebrew is described as desolate, barren and lonely.[2] So by comparing both of these definitions, we can easily summarize a wilderness experience as:

1. very lonely (uninhabited),
2. unfruitful and barren (uncultivated and desolate),
3. dry (having little or no water; thirsty),
4. wild (*wild*erness; roving; wandering and untamed like a wild animal),
5. filled with disorder.

Can you relate to these descriptions? Have you felt lonely, barren and unfruitful? Have you been so dry and thirsty that you found yourself crying out to God in desperation? Is your life in disorder? Are you at times confused and irritated? Have you responded to your circumstances with *wild* behavior while in your *wild*erness?

If you can relate, then read on.

Do not remain discouraged! Certainly God has a purpose for your wilderness, but He does not plan for you to stay there.

The Slavery Mentality

Just like He has a purpose for your wilderness, God had a purpose for allowing the Israelites to wander in their wilderness. God brought the Israelites out of Egypt not only for the purpose of proving their hearts, but also to give them the opportunity to be delivered from a slavery mentality.

While in the wilderness, the Israelites had many opportunities to activate their faith for their breakthroughs, but instead they remained in the slavery mentality of the past. Many times their response was to blame Moses for their circumstances rather than trust God at greater levels. The wilderness was chosen by God to be their road to deliverance, yet because of their incorrect responses, they remained in their wilderness longer than God ever intended. The Israelites could not break free from their lack of trust in God or their lack of trust in Moses, and they remained in a place of total surrender to old thoughts and behavior patterns. It took them forty years to break free from the slavery mentality of the past and leave their wilderness.

Although you might not immediately recognize slavery behavior in your own life, let me explain what the term *slave* actually means. In the spiritual sense, it is described as bondage, in which one experiences a form of imprisonment and captivity. It is also a type of restraint of one's liberty and a lack of empowerment to become "free." A slave also is described as a person who has no will of his own and is wholly under the control of another. Another definition describes a slave as one who surrenders himself to any power whatsoever—for instance, a slave to passion, lust or ambition.

Does this sound familiar to you? Could this be where you are right now? Is there any sin that controls you? Do you suffer with any type of bondage from which you cannot break free? God desires to set you free, and He will sometimes allow a wilderness to provoke you into activating your faith to break free from your situation.

Old Cycles

The reason the Israelites remained in the wilderness is because they never cycled out of a slavery mentality. The Israelites were tested many times in their faith and motives. Because they could not totally trust God, they remained in their wilderness—and they died there. God allowed the old generation to die in the wilderness, and He raised up an entirely new generation to go into the Promised Land. Their old cycles prevented them from moving into the new thing God had planned for them.

Most of the modern prophets agree that the Church today is in a spiritual season in which God is exposing old cycles. Most likely you have felt that you are simply continuing to "go around the same mountain again." This phrase implies confronting the same past issues over and over again. Some of these are generational patterns of behavior. In fact, the word *generation* implies a continuing cycle or circle.

Another implication for generational patterns is the use of the word *always*. Have you ever thought, or even stated out loud, "Well, I have *always* been this way. I can't change! It will *always* be as it is now."

God is declaring that it is time to cycle out of old patterns and past generational behavior. I want to go into the Promised Land, don't you? In order to do so, we must be determined to cycle out of our doubt and unbelief, religious mind-sets, generational strongholds and whatever else so easily besets us.

Our Faith and Character Are Tested in the Wilderness

No one asks for a wilderness experience, and we most likely do not pray to God to send us to the wilderness. So why do we find ourselves in the wilderness? And once we are there, how do we get out?

Well, when it is God who sends us there, we must embrace the season in humility and faith. By this I mean that we are to submit to His purpose as He proves us and allow our faith to be developed while in the wilderness.

I know it might challenge someone's theology when I say that many times it is God who sends us into a dry, desolate place. Although there are seasons when Satan attempts to illegally cover us with darkness and cause us to experience desolation and hopelessness, we cannot always blame a wilderness experience on the devil. After all, Jesus was led by the Spirit to His wilderness (see Luke 4) to be tempted by Satan. It was not the devil who led Him; it was God who led Jesus to the dry place. Why? It was Jesus' victory over the demonic temptations that helped empower Him for the miraculous.

The word *tempted* translates "to try, to prove and to examine."[3] It also is translated to imply that Jesus was actually "on trial" to prove what He believed. It was a time when Jesus' faith, virtue and character were tested to prove His character and steadfastness. In His desert experience, Jesus grew even stronger in His faith and gave the devil a black eye at the same time.

It is the same with us. When we go through wilderness times, our virtue, faith and character are tested. It is through these times of testing that we truly recognize our responses—whether they are responses of faith or of doubt and unbelief—our hidden motives of the heart and our hidden attitudes. If there are any hidden selfish motives, ungodly beliefs and attitudes or impure responses, they need to be exposed and addressed so that we can reach the next level of breakthrough.

Know this for certain: The tempter will come with his evil seductions, but if our responses are right, we will overcome temptation and be stronger after we have endured the fire.

"The Proceeding Word"

While He was in the wilderness, Jesus developed what I refer to as a "proceeding word." A proceeding word is the Word of God that is proclaimed to the enemy when we are tempted to come into a negative agreement with the devil. An example of a "proceeding word" can be seen when Jesus proclaimed to Satan, "Man does not live on bread alone, but on every word that comes [proceeds] from the mouth of God" (Matthew 4:4).

Proceeding words are God-given declarations based on the Word of God that flow from our innermost being. Like a mighty river, God's Word should gush forth from our mouths whenever we are in a wilderness and the enemy is tempting us. God is seeking a people who allow themselves to be developed in the wilderness so that they become empowered with these proceeding words.

Rather than feeling sorry for ourselves because we experience dry places, we must realize that God has a much greater plan. He is empowering us for the miraculous and for "greater things"!

Most prophets are declaring that the Church is entering into a season of apostolic signs and wonders. In order for us to believe and receive miracles for ourselves and others, we must develop a proceeding word. We must know and understand the Word of God. In addition, we must rid ourselves of religious mind-sets concerning the miraculous. We must flow by His Spirit and allow Him to move when He desires. Timing is very important when following the Holy Spirit. He moves in His own timing, and we must develop a hearing ear to recognize when He directs us. Developing a spiritual sensitivity is crucial as we fully embrace the Kingdom message.

Tests for Promotion

In my own life, I have observed that whenever God is planning to move me to a higher spiritual level, I usually go through a wilderness experience. I feel I am going through a dark tunnel—I cannot see clearly. I am spiritually dry and, therefore, crying out for a breakthrough. In other words, I get desperate for God.

In the midst of all of this, God is watching and listening to all of my responses. He is testing my heart, my motives and my responses. When I do not have all the "right" responses, I find myself repenting. I begin to come out of the wilderness when I firmly develop that "proceeding word." In other words, the Word of God becomes firm and solid in my spirit, and my response to the devil is to quote the Word of God and my prophetic promises. To my amazement, although I feel I do not deserve it, God promotes me. (Thank God for His amazing grace!) Once I am out of the wilderness and flowing again in the Spirit, I look back and thank the Lord for the lesson in spiritual maturity. This is what I commonly refer to as "promotion in the Spirit."

I believe the Church is in a season in which God is testing our hearts, motives and responses because He desires to promote us. Whenever we desire to grow, have a more effective ministry and extend the Kingdom of God, we face tests of promotion. It is as if we are students in the "School of the Holy Spirit," and a test of promotion is one of the most difficult tests to pass.

But once we pass it and are on the other side of the test, we look back and see that we have been promoted. We have arrived at a greater spiritual level. When Jesus endured forty days of fasting and the difficult temptations He faced, He came out of His wilderness experience in victory with power and might. This is God's goal for us, as well—that we leave our wilderness in victory, moving in the power and might of His Spirit and doing greater works for His Kingdom than we were doing before.

Some of you are in the wilderness, and God wants to cycle you out. The way to come out is to realize that God is seeking a proceeding word. Give it! He wants to promote you and use you in a mighty way. Make sure you are ready for it! You might come out for a while and then find yourself back in another test. If so, just begin to cycle out again with another proceeding word. While we are in the wilderness, we are to grow and mature and have His Word so impregnated in our spirits that we come forth in power and might.

Breaking Free of a Slavery Mentality

There is one surefire way to cycle out of your slavery mentality: Begin to speak what God says about you. Remember all your prophetic promises and begin to proclaim what God has said. At every test, use a proceeding word to break out of your captivity.

A slave mentality says that God will not fulfill His Word. The proceeding word is that He promises to perform His Word.

A slave mentality says that you will not find your place in ministry. The proceeding word is that God has firmly planted you into your destiny and you will not be plucked up.

Closely examine every ungodly belief and replace it with God's Word, and then you will experience your deliverance. When you begin to respond to every wilderness test with a proceeding word spoken in faith, you will cycle out of your captivity.

Cutting the Umbilical Cord of the Past

Crossing over into our place of destiny requires action on our part. Yes, Jesus shed His precious blood for our freedom, deliverance and healing. But we must make a firm decision to cut the cords to the past so that we may be empowered to cross over into our promises.

When the Israelites were set free from Pharaoh and the bondage of Egypt, they were cut loose from all that they had known. They left the only life they had ever experienced, but their belief systems were still based on their past experiences. They were unable to cut free completely from the past. Ezekiel 16:2–5 speaks of an umbilical cord that had held Israel in bondage for generations:

> "Son of man, cause Jerusalem to know her abominations, and say, 'Thus says the Lord GOD to Jerusalem: "Your birth and your nativity are from the land of Canaan; your father was an Amorite and your mother a Hittite. As for your nativity, on the day you were born your navel cord was not cut, nor were you washed in water to cleanse you; you were not rubbed with salt nor wrapped in swaddling cloths. No eye pitied you, to do any of these things for you, to have compassion on you; but you were thrown out into the open field, when you yourself were loathed on the day you were born."'"
>
> Ezekiel 16:2–5, NKJV

In the natural, an umbilical cord is a type of feeding mechanism. It is the cord that keeps a baby alive by providing nourishment. But the cord is meant to be cut at the proper time of birthing. When a child is born, there must be a "cutting of the cord." This means that the cord to the old system of life and nourishment is severed. The child becomes a living, breathing being on its own. The child cannot grow properly unless the cord is cut.

In the spiritual realm, there is also a cord that must be cut—the cord to the past. This means that we must no longer rely on belief systems that are based upon past experiences, but instead we must receive life from the breath of God and His words only.

When Israel left Egypt, it was the proper time for her cord to be cut. But Israel was never able to totally cut the umbilical cord to the past, and as a result her people did not enter into their land of promise. Only two men of faith, Joshua and Caleb, actually crossed over fully into the Promised Land. Joshua led an entirely new generation into Canaan; the old generation died in the wilderness.

It is also important to note that the blood within the umbilical cord is known as "cord blood." New medical research is now using these cord blood cells for bone-marrow transplants. This is extremely interesting because, as we discussed in chapter 5, bones represent structure. Spiritually, when He cuts a cord to the past, God is restructuring our lives, our churches, our businesses, our families—indeed, everything that concerns us!

Cutting the cord to old generational bloodlines is very important so that we can move forward with the power of the blood of Jesus. Taking a covenant meal—Holy Communion—reminds us of the tremendous sacrifice Jesus paid with His own blood, and now He is our umbilical cord to life.

What is holding you captive? Why can't you move forward in faith? Are you holding on to cords to the past? Is it God's time to cut them? Is your spirit challenged to move from your past and cross over into your destiny?

Dear ones, it is time to cut the cords to the past. We must lock into what God says, digest His words and cross over into our Land of Promise!

The Amorite and Hittite Strongholds

In the Ezekiel passage previously quoted, notice that the Lord mentions that the father was an Amorite and the mother a Hittite. This is a metaphor that refers to the iniquity of generational strongholds and patterns—umbilical cords to the past that need to be cut.

The name *Amorite* is a Hebrew name meaning "a mountaineer, a talker or a slayer."[4] If any of us places the devil's words above God's words, then Satan has a seated position, or a higher place. And if we heed Satan's words, then he can easily slay us. Is the enemy talking to you? Are you listening? As a result, does the enemy have a high place in your life? In other words, does Satan have any seated position over you? This is just one example of how a person may still be tied to an old umbilical cord to the past.

The name *Hittite* is a Hebrew word meaning "an annoyer, dread or fear."[5] The word *annoy* means "troublesome or bothersome."[6] There are many different forms that the spirit of fear will attempt to manifest in order to annoy us and cause us dread. Do you have a dread of your future? Does fear have a seated position in your life? Are you annoyed with fears of failure, fears of abandonment, fear of death or fear of rejection? What continues to bother or trouble you? It is quite possible that the umbilical cord to a past fear needs to be cut.

As we go through this season, the Lord desires to shift us out of bondage. It is time to come out of old structures of iniquity. *Iniquity* means "bent over."[7] Many of us have "bent" thinking concerning God and His ability to lead us. Do we really trust God? Will He do what He says He will do?

Cut the cords to the Amorite and the Hittite in your past. Allow God to lead you, and trust in His power and might to bring you into the destiny He has planned for you.

The Fear of Abandonment

The Ezekiel passage also makes clear that many of us face abandonment issues—issues of rejection because of an old "tie" to the past. Notice that the Lord was referring to a child's umbilical cord never being cut; the child was never washed, cleansed or covered (wrapped in clothing). Notice also that the baby did not feel pitied (he felt that no one cared). This opened the door for a deep wounding, and the child was receptive to abandonment issues—never feeling loved, nurtured and protected. Shame becomes a stronghold when a child is raised with these feelings.

Many of us fear abandonment. Abandonment issues manifest because of generational patterns of iniquity, generational bloodlines and old religious belief systems that set us up for failure. Thankfully, knowing that we are grafted into God's family assures us that we belong to God.

The Spirit of Religion

Religion keeps us from moving into the new.[8] Religion states that we must continue to "prove" our worthiness, which is *not* scriptural. With a spirit of religion, we will never measure up. Maintaining a tie to a religious spirit is the same as holding onto an umbilical cord to the past. It is another thing that keeps us from moving out of our wilderness.

We do not have to prove ourselves with religious works; we have been bought with a price. Christ's blood is our umbilical cord, and we belong to Him because He has purchased us.

Cut the Cords to the Past and Move Out of the Wilderness!

As long as an old umbilical cord—food from our past—is connected, we will not become empowered to leave the wilderness and cross over. Part of crossing over involves embracing a fresh move of God's Spirit and allowing Him to lead us down pathways that are new and unfamiliar. Will you allow God to remake you into a new wineskin? Will you allow Him to cut the umbilical cord to your past? Are you ready to fully follow Him and cross over?

If you are ready to be cut loose from Egypt, then take some time for the Lord to speak to you, and then go through a time of repentance. Rise up, anoint yourself, anoint the doorpost of your heart and declare that you will move forward with God into your new place.

Following are some steps that will help you cut the cords to the past and move out of the wilderness. (It is okay to take some baby steps through this!)

- Close your eyes and imagine yourself as a baby who is about to take his first step on his own. One step, two steps, three steps . . . and now you are moving forward. You did it! Although you may have to stabilize yourself with the nearby coffee table or someone's hand, you have now cut the cord to the past. You have conquered your fear of the unknown. Did you see yourself grabbing a hand along the way? Jesus is there to help you through this process! List below the fears you face as you let go.

- What victories will you gain as you remove yourself from that old place of fear, doubt and unbelief? List them below.

- Are there any relationships that hold you back? How do they influence you to remain in old patterns of behavior? What are your plans to "let go"? List these below.

- By listing below the very best things that will happen if you fully let go, you will gain vision for your future. List your future steps for the best!

- Take some time to read Luke 18:28–30. Pray and meditate over what Jesus said about letting go.

Prayer of Release from the Past

Father, I realize that it is now my time to move forward. I recognize that I am still tied to my past. I confess that I have not been fed fully by Your Holy Spirit. I repent for believing lies from the enemy. I choose to believe what Your Word says concerning me, my family and anything else in my life (state names, businesses, ministries, etc.). I choose to digest only Your Word, and I will feast upon Your words of life in the days to come. I ask that You sever the umbilical cord to my past. I believe that Jesus Christ was born to destroy the works of Satan, that He died on the cross for my sins and that He sits at Your right hand, so I know that I am in right standing with You. I receive my new measure of life today. Thank You for the blood of Jesus that washes me white as snow and cleanses me from past mistakes and all unrighteousness. Today I thank You that I am connected to You. I am fed daily by You and Your Word. In Jesus' mighty name, Amen!

8/16/08

8

STIRRING UP TROUBLE

Ahab went to meet Elijah. When he saw Elijah, he said to him, "Is that you, you *troubler* of Israel?"

"I have not made trouble for Israel," Elijah replied. "But you and your father's family have. You have abandoned the LORD's commands and have followed the Baals."

1 Kings 18:16–18, emphasis mine

He seems to just show up on the scene one day. He is Elijah, the Tishbite, from a town called Gilead.

Now how could someone with a handle of "Tishbite" actually ever cause any "trouble" to the devil? "Tishbite" sounds more like an infectious insect's sting than a man with a mantle of authority. But this one man with a strange name caused so much of a stir in Israel that he was used to usher in one of the most powerful miraculous demonstrations in biblical history.

Elijah

The name *Elijah* translates as "God is Jehovah."[1] As I stated before, *Jehovah* represents the "God of our future." Elijah's name actually could be considered as God's prophetic action released through Elijah's deeds. Being a prophet and keenly aware of the plans and purposes of Jehovah, Elijah could sense the breakthroughs of the future, as well as prophesy the release of that future.

Elijah was considered one of the greatest of the prophets. He is what I would refer to as one of God's "Bravehearts." He was an Old Testament prophet who truly desired to see heaven come to earth. In fact, at his death, heaven did come to earth. A chariot of fire hurled from heaven and took Elijah up in a whirlwind.

Elijah had a heart to experience God's greatness, and he moved forward with bravery and courage. Being brave and courageous does not mean an absence of fear. No! In fact, facing fearful situations actually causes our faith to become more courageous. Courage looks fear in the eye and says, "Move aside. I've got territory to conquer for God!"

First Kings 17 first mentions Elijah and tells of his initial season of ministry:

> Now Elijah the Tishbite, from Tishbe in Gilead, said to Ahab, "As the LORD, the God of Israel, lives, whom I serve, there will be neither dew nor rain in the next few years except at *my* word."
>
> 1 Kings 17:1, emphasis mine

In this chapter alone, Elijah prophesied drought, was supernaturally fed by ravens and heard from God as to where to go for divine provision. In his ministry, Elijah pressed through obstacles numerous times to gain victory. He faced many challenges—challenges with natural circumstances, as well as with people. One of the biggest challenges, in my opinion, was to have faith that what he prophesied would actually come to pass. Think about it: Prophesying that there would be no rain unless he said so—now that is a big faith statement. This prophet had nerve!

Elijah challenged not only natural circumstances but also the faith of others. He actually ordered a poor widow to feed him her last meal. He showed up in Zarephath, stopped at the gate of the city and then commanded a widow to serve him some water—and she did it! Now that in itself is amazing because she did not even know who he was at the time.

But not only did she give him a drink, she also gave him her last meal when he commanded her to do so. This poor, starving widow neglected her own hunger and her son's hunger, and she fed the prophet with her last morsel of bread. Prepared to die herself, she cared for the man of God. Talk about laying down your life for a higher purpose! By her obedience to the prophet's directive, the widow's meals were multiplied.

Later, the widow's son became sick and died. Because of the woman's faith and the faith and obedience of Elijah, the boy was raised from the dead. Elijah's obedience to God's will supernaturally positioned him to be used by God to perform a miracle. Think of how awesome this miracle was: The breath of heaven came to earth and brought life to a dead child. Now that is what I call heaven touching earth! The breath of God filled that young boy's lungs through the obedience of a prophet. I pray that we all can be used in that dimension for His glory.

Bless Elijah's Brave Heart!

For many of us, all of this would be enough to prove our dedication and commitment to God and give us the courage to overcome obstacles along the way. But Elijah was on a mission of bravery; he was about to confront strong demonic powers of darkness that were seducing God's people into sin and apostasy.

In chapter 18, Elijah met Ahab. It had been three years since there had been any rain. Ahab had been on a quest to find water, and he summoned Obadiah, a God-fearing man, to help him. Jezebel, Ahab's wife, had just murdered one hundred prophets of God and would have killed another fifty if Obadiah had not hidden them in a cave for protection. So when God told Elijah to go and show himself to Ahab, it was like telling one of us to go and show ourselves to the devil himself (see 1 Kings 18:1–6). Dear ones, that took bravery!

When Ahab saw Elijah, he asked, "Are you the guy who is stirring up so much trouble?" (see 1 Kings 18:17). Ahab blamed God's prophet for the drought rather than admit that his own sin had released God's judgment upon Israel. Isn't that just like the devil—blinding people to their own sin and then blaming the prophets for their outcome?

Elijah boldly responded by reminding Ahab that it was not he who was causing such a stir. The problem was with Ahab and Ahab's father's sins. They had forsaken God's commandments and followed Baal. Ahab had not only disobeyed God's commandments, but he also embraced his wife's false gods. Jezebel had introduced idolatrous worship into Israel, along with her false prophets.

> Ahab went to meet Elijah. When he saw Elijah, he said to him, "Is that you, you troubler of Israel?"
>
> "I have not made trouble for Israel," Elijah replied. "But you and your father's family have. You have abandoned the LORD's commands and have followed the Baals. Now summon the people from all over Israel to meet me on Mount Carmel. And bring the four hundred and fifty prophets of Baal and the four hundred prophets of Asherah, who eat at Jezebel's table." So Ahab sent

word throughout all Israel and assembled the prophets on Mount Carmel.

1 Kings 18:16–20

Elijah then confronted the people of Israel and challenged them to follow the one true God. When the people did not answer, Elijah challenged the 450 false prophets to a confrontation on Mount Carmel. He called down fire from heaven to prove God's power and faithfulness. Afterward, he slew the 450 false prophets at the brook of Kishon, he rose up and prophesied the rain to commence, and on top of that, he girded up his loins and outran Ahab's chariot into Jezreel!

Bless his heart—I wonder if he realized that his prophetic calling would require so much?

On the Devil's Hit List

Truly heaven touched earth, a miracle occurred and Elijah had his name in lights. This was truly a death-to-self mission that Elijah had accomplished. But the confrontations were not over.

Elijah soon found his name on the devil's hit list. When a person is determined to shift out of the old and embrace the Kingdom message, praying that God's will be done on earth, the devil does not lie down and roll over like a whipped puppy dog. When we get serious about establishing God's Kingdom on earth, the devil also becomes serious about us.

Elijah had confronted the false god and the false prophets—but not Jezebel! Now for the real test of bravery: Elijah had to face the brazen woman who was so defiling to Israel that God rebuked anyone who gave place to her teachings. (In my book *Destiny Thieves*, I discuss the spirit of Jezebel and how this evil seducing stronghold can rob us of our destiny.)

When faced with Jezebel's intimidation and her threats to kill him (see 1 Kings 19:1–2), Elijah lost his vision and ran in fear. "And when he *saw that*, he arose, and went for his life, and came to Beersheba, which belongeth to Judah, and left his servant there" (1 Kings 19:3, KJV, emphasis mine). Because Elijah "saw" his death in his mind, he ran.

Persecuted by Jezebel's threats, Elijah took off, running away from his position of authority. God had already established Elijah's authority in the land. But when faced with heavy persecution, Elijah tossed his breakthroughs to the side, ran into the wilderness and hid in a cave. He was so discouraged that he even wished to die.

Elijah was not supposed to leave the scene. Elijah was to remain and defeat Jezebel. Instead he took off, running away from her. What had happened to his bravery? What had affected his heart for fulfilling God's plan for his life?

Isn't it amazing how powerful a Jezebel spirit can be? That demonic power, which is connected to divination and witchcraft, actually brings so much persecution against us that we develop an inward vision of defeat and then take off, running into the wilderness and hiding from our call and destiny—even wishing to die.

God had to call Elijah out of hiding and recommission him. God told him to go back, face Jezebel and fulfill his destiny.

"What Are You Doing Here in This Cave?"

Has God ever asked you to do something you deemed so difficult that you could not in your wildest imagination "see" yourself doing it? Did you ever find yourself feeling totally incapable of completing all God requires? Was it possibly because you lost your vision? How important it is for us not only to have a vision, but also to maintain the vision! Far too often, our vision gets stolen. In fact, many times it is a Jezebel spirit that robs us of the vision.[2]

Like Elijah, my prophetic discernment easily stirs up trouble. When I travel, I frequently address territorial strongholds that adversely affect churches, regions and individuals. As a result, demons are stirred up and begin to manifest. Often I feel I am in double trouble due to the spiritual attacks I begin to experience. Fear grips my heart, I feel intimidated and insecure, and I want to run away from my next assignment. More times than I care to admit, I have actually run and hidden. The challenge to rise up and face false accusers in my defense is at times overwhelming. Rather than rising up and advancing forward, I sometimes withdraw into complacency and travel an easier road of "spiritual maintenance." This highway seems less threatening, but it does not open doors to fresh revelation and breakthroughs. It is only a matter of time before I feel dry and spiritually hungry and find myself crying out for more of His glory.

Then I hear God say, *Sandie, what are you doing here in this cave? Do you think you can hide from Me?*

"No, God," I say, "I am not hiding from You. I am hiding from the persecution!"

Then He says, *No, you are hiding from Me and what I have called you to do. Now get up and go back to regain the ground you have lost, for there is still much to do.*

The Power of Persecution

When we run from persecution, we think we are running from the devil. But in actuality we are running from God.

Persecution is a tool the enemy uses to deflate our faith and determination. It is easy to speak of heaven touching earth when we are under a strong anointing. Prophesying God's words over people and allowing the words of heaven to penetrate their future is awesome! But every prophetic word is tried and tested—and so is the one giving the words.

Daniel 7 teaches us how the enemy destroys us with persecution:

> He shall speak pompous words against the Most High, shall *persecute* the saints of the Most High, and shall intend to change times and law. Then the saints shall be given into his hand for a time and times and half a time.
>
> verse 25, NKJV, emphasis mine

The Aramaic word for "persecute" is *belah*, which means to "wear out the mind."[3] If the enemy can attack our minds and cause fear, doubt and unbelief, then we are soon at the point where we easily lose courage and faith and possibly run in the opposite direction of divine fulfillment.

Imagine the intense pressure and mind games Elijah must have faced! Through persecution, the devil tried to destroy Elijah's destiny by changing his times and seasons. Daniel 2:21 tells us that "[God] changeth the times and the seasons" (KJV). But Satan "shall persecute the saints of the Most High, and shall intend to change times and law" (Daniel 7:25, NKJV). He attempts to roll back our predetermined breakthroughs—our destinies—by persecuting us to the point that we quit before our appointed times of breakthrough. He causes us to run away from our source of blessing. God wanted to bless Elijah right where he was. Just because Jezebel rose up and threatened to kill Elijah did not mean that God would not have used Elijah to call down fire upon her head—right where she was. But, instead of asking God what to do, Elijah took off running in fear.

The Solution: Renew the Mind

The solution to persecution is to renew the mind. Because persecution involves wearing out the mind, then we must renew our minds so that we do not become worn down.

I beseech you therefore, brethren, by the mercies of God, that you present your bodies a living sacrifice, holy, acceptable to God, which is your reasonable service. And do not be conformed to this world, but be transformed by the renewing of your mind, that you may prove what is that good and acceptable and perfect will of God.

Romans 12:1–2, NKJV

Notice that Romans 12:2 refers to being "transformed." Transformation is a metamorphosis experience, as when a worm endures the process of transforming into a beautiful butterfly. To completely renew our minds and neutralize the power of persecution, we must embrace change. We must change the way we think, becoming totally open to whatever God desires for us to do.

When I find myself in situations where I want to run and hide, I have to renew my mind and allow God to change my heart. I have to regain my vision, get my heart right with the Lord and resubmit to His plan for my life. To do this, I must face fears, rise up in courage, move forward to fulfill a new assignment and get back in the race.

If you have been like me, running in the opposite direction from where you should be, then consider yourself in good company! Elijah was one of the most powerful prophets in the Bible, and he also heard God say, *What are you doing here in this cave?*

Precious saints, we will not be able to see heaven's plans touch and change this earth without spiritual warfare. The devil will not give up his position of authority so easily. But if we remain focused and press past old paradigms that limit God's ability to empower us, then we will experience major breakthroughs and witness His Kingdom coming. Let's get up, go back to where we should be and regain what was lost. Let's get in the race with a faster pace!

Will You Be a Braveheart?

Elijah's first response was fear, but through the renewing of his mind, he embraced change and responded in faith—a true and victorious Braveheart.

Do you need to renew your mind today? I encourage you to face your weakness and ask God what responses need to change. Listed below are some strategies from heaven's throne that will empower you to renew your mind and keep you moving forward, opening heaven's doors for transformation to occur.

- Realize that you can only move forward when you fully embrace the truth of God's Word. The Scripture exhorts us to "let this mind be in you which was also in Christ Jesus" (Philippians 2:5, NKJV). Ask the Lord to give you the mind of Christ. List the open doors that allow your mind to be influenced in a negative way (movies, books, pornography, poor relationships, etc.), and then ask God to forgive you for allowing demonic entrance.

- Romans 12:1–2 is the main Scripture passage concerning renewing the mind. The renewal process begins with presenting our bodies as a living sacrifice. Take some time in prayer and offer yourself in service to the Lord. Then ask Him to empower you to keep His instructions holy and separated unto Him. Finally, separate yourself from situations that bring defilement.

- Be honest with God. Admit to the Lord that you need to renew your mind. Tell Him your thoughts—He knows them anyway. Then repent and change.

- Pray this prayer with me:

    Father God, in the precious name of Jesus, I choose to accept Your invitation to change. I have decided to let go of my past fears and embrace my future. I confess that my mind needs renewing and that I have harbored evil thoughts. I also confess that I have allowed a fear of the future to cause me to run from my calling and destiny. I desire to experience all the joy You have for me, which includes the joy of serving You. I want to experience the strength of Your transforming power that will propel me forward in every way. I yield to Your desire to change my heart, my mind, my ministry and my life. And even though I may face persecution, I will count it all joy because my strength is in You. In Jesus' name, Amen.

9

JUMPING INTO THE RIVER

Then the angel showed me the river of the water of life, as clear as crystal, flowing from the throne of God and of the Lamb.

Revelation 22:1

Have you ever driven your car to a destination and, once you arrived, realized that you could not remember how you got there? *Where was my mind while I was driving? I could have had an accident!* I am always amazed at how faithful the Lord is to protect us even when we are not using wisdom.

One Friday night, while I was driving to our "First Friday Fire" church service, I was totally "caught up" in an open vision. I lost all sensing in the natural; yet I was under the Lord's protective care while still behind the wheel of the car. Maybe the Holy Ghost was driving; all I know is that I arrived to the meeting fully intact.

While on the way to the service, I had prayed a simple prayer. I asked that we would be led totally by His Spirit during every meeting. I promised to have open ears to hear His divine direction by laying down my own agenda, mind-sets and religious paradigms. *God, I want only You,* I reminded Him, *so please equip me with Your sevenfold Spirit to ensure that I do not grieve You.* I know that I can cross over into my Promised Land only if I am equipped by His Spirit. I can hear properly only when I totally depend upon Him. I know that unless I go first to His throne room to receive instruction and strategy, I can be influenced easily by an old voice—one that speaks to me out of a mind-set that limits God.

The vision God gave me that evening was the direct result of that prayer.

The Vision of the River of God

In the vision, I saw the River of God, and it was incredibly wide. I was not concerned with how deep it was; I was simply amazed at its width. It appeared so wide that I knew many could be in His River at once.

Now I understand why I was shown the River's true dimension. I had been narrow-minded concerning God's Church. Even in the vision, I was talking to myself, wondering why I had limited the width of His River!

His Church is a many-membered Body of believers that is not limited to a particular denomination, religious camp or race. His Kingdom encompasses all who believe in Christ Jesus as the Son of God and who believe that His blood was shed for the remission of our sins. Our narrow-mindedness has caused religious pride and prejudice, which negates the fullness of the Kingdom message. God's Kingdom is a kingdom for "whosoever": "Whosoever shall call on the name of the Lord shall be saved"

(Acts 2:21, KJV). These "whosoever" people are those who follow after God through their personal relationship with Christ Jesus. They are the believers who deny themselves and choose to follow Him (see Mark 8:34–35).

The River of God was also a constant flow, always active and moving. It was fresh, clean and clear. It was such an awesome sight; I wanted so much to jump in and experience the life it contained. In this vision, however, I was allowed only to observe its majestic presence. The River seemed to be a testimony that stood entirely upon its own merit, as if it possessed its own identity. This River also had its own voice and made a constant sound as if it spoke throughout eternity. Its sound continued to flow forth the entire time of my observation. Yet at the same time, it represented and fully emanated all that the Godhead is in its fullness. It was a River of Life that cleansed and released joy, as well as abounding love. I was now aware that He, God Himself, was the River!

Suddenly I was able to view the waters more closely and noticed a glittering, gold-like substance that seemed to reflect into the atmosphere. Then I noticed the mouth of the River, from which all sounds came. I became aware that the mouth was also the throne of God. The throne was both the mouth and the head—the beginning—of the entire River of God. Its color was a brilliant, blazing gold throne, and its intense illumination seemed to completely overshadow the flow of the River, causing a liquid gold substance to flow throughout its entire course.

The golden throne, with its blazing brilliance, seemed to melt into the River, as if they became one. Yet it never melted into nothingness because the throne was alive and full of power and activity. The brilliance seemed to be from an intense fire that was never quenched, yet that melted a golden substance into the waters.

Then a different brilliance caught my eye. I was allowed to move closer, so that I could actually put my hands in these waters. I saw a very clear sparkle, and I bent over to attempt to pick up what seemed to be diamonds. Although I never picked one from these waters, I knew that what I was seeing were diamonds.

I asked the Lord what this meant, and He said the diamonds were symbolic of marriage and covenant. He went on to explain that the more intimate we become with Him, the more we are able to swim in these waters.

Then the vision ended. But it had birthed a prophetic message inside my spirit.

Revelation 22 Describes His River of Life

Revelation 22 explains God's awesome River of Life. This River once flowed at the beginning of time in the Garden of Eden, yet we lost access to it because of sin. The River that flowed through the Garden of Eden is documented in the book of Genesis, but before we discuss it, we will carefully examine the River of Life in Revelation 22. As you read through the following passage, be sure to heed the emphasized words. Also notice that the Tree of Life is mentioned several times, as this will be significant later in our study.

> And he showed me a *pure river of water of life*, clear as crystal, proceeding *from the throne* of God and of the Lamb. In the middle of its street, and on either side of the river, *was the tree of life*, which bore twelve fruits, each tree yielding its fruit every month. The leaves of the tree were for the *healing of the nations*. And there shall be *no more curse*, but the throne of God and of the Lamb shall be in it, and His servants shall serve Him. *They shall see His face*, and His name shall be on their foreheads. There shall be no night there: They need no lamp nor light of the sun, *for the Lord God gives them light*. And *they shall reign forever and ever*.

Then he said to me, "These words are faithful and true." And the Lord God of the holy prophets sent His angel to show His servants the things which must shortly take place.

"Behold, I am coming quickly! Blessed is he who keeps the words of the prophecy of this book."

Now I, John, saw and heard these things. And when I heard and saw, I fell down to worship before the feet of the angel who showed me these things.

Then he said to me, "See that you do not do that. For I am your fellow servant, and of your brethren the prophets, and of those who keep the words of this book. Worship God." And he said to me, "Do not seal the words of the prophecy of this book, for the time is at hand. He who is unjust, let him be unjust still; he who is filthy, let him be filthy still; he who is righteous, let him be righteous still; he who is holy, let him be holy still."

"And behold, I am coming quickly, and My reward is with Me, to give to every one according to his work. I am the Alpha and the Omega, the Beginning and the End, the First and the Last."

Blessed are those who do His commandments, that *they may have the right to the tree of life, and may enter through the gates into the city.*

Revelation 22:1–14, NKJV, emphasis mine

The Scripture assures us that as we remain in His River and before His throne, these covenant promises are fulfilled in our lives:

1. We receive life.
2. We eat of the fruit of the land. (By being in the River we are in a place of fulfilled promise.)
3. We can experience healing.
4. We are delivered from any curses (a curse of death, barrenness, sickness and disease, poverty—any and every curse).
5. We are positioned to see Him.

6. We experience the Light; there is no more darkness as God gives us light.
7. We have authority to rule and reign, taking dominion over our circumstances.
8. We have entrance through the gates (the ability to go through any gate into our new season of breakthrough).

According to this passage, if we believe what has been written (verses 7–9) and remain properly positioned, then we have all these covenant blessings and promises. The Alpha and Omega, the Beginning and the End, spoke this revelation to John, and it should be kept "holy" before the Lord. In other words, this is holy ground to God; tuck this revelation deep into your heart and stay properly positioned.

The Apostolic Dimension in the River of God

To receive the fullness of the revelation concerning the River of God, we must go back to the beginning. First things need to be first.

In an apostolic reformation, where apostolic authority is being reinstated to the earth, the apostles reestablish God's truths. This is not to say that God's truths ever ceased, but rather that there is a "building-upon" process. Reformation means that we must build upon past revelation. We are not throwing an old foundation away; we are adding to the previous revelation and understanding. I refer to this process as moving from glory to glory (see 2 Corinthians 3:18). When we are properly positioned at the throne—in His River—a greater level of glory is experienced, along with greater faith to embrace and walk out the new revelation. In essence, we are building our faith upon our previous faith. Our faith is extended into greater dimensions because of the expanded revelation.

Isn't this exciting? Are you ready for another launch? Hold on, here we go!

Alpha: The Beginning

Genesis 1 is the documentation of the Alpha part of God: the Beginning. In this chapter the Creator spoke His entire creation into existence. The heavens, the earth, all creatures, animals and waters became God's palette of beauty and life.

The creation process from our Alpha God flows into chapter 2 of Genesis, in which He fashioned a man from the dust of the earth, gave him a companion and breathed life into them both. Created in God's own image, Adam and Eve were given total dominion upon the earth. Then He blessed them and commanded them to be fruitful and multiply. Thus was the beginning of God's covenant promise to each of us.

We, too, have been created in His image and have been given power and authority. We are commanded to be fruitful and multiply, and we are fellow partakers of His covenant blessings.

In this beginning book, we are told that the Tree of Life is found in the Garden of Eden. Remember that in the book of Revelation, the last book of the Bible, there is also the mention of a Tree of Life. We see, therefore, that the Tree of Life was meant to be available to us from the very beginning of time. When mankind sinned, we lost access to the Tree of Life, and, therefore, Christ had to redeem life for us. By swimming in the River from God's throne, we can experience the fullness of life and His promise.

The River in the Garden of Eden

There is also mention of a river in the Garden of Eden. This river was a type and shadow of the River that flowed from God's throne (see Revelation 22). Mankind was never to leave his original home; the paradise of Eden had every blessing possible. Everything lived. Fruitfulness, blessings and life abundant thrived in the Garden where the river flowed! Although mankind was driven out of the Garden and away from this river, these refreshing waters have since been restored to us through the blood of Christ. Jesus died that we might have life (see John 10:10). We have full access, therefore, to swim in the River of Life. Hallelujah!

This river flowed through the Garden and then parted into four heads. The river went through the fruitful areas, just as the River of God in Revelation 22 produced fruit and life. Because we are building upon past revelation, let's closely examine the four heads of the river in the Garden to gain greater understanding.

> And a river went out of Eden to water the garden; and from thence it was parted, and became into four heads. The name of the first is Pison: that is it which compasseth the whole land of Havilah, where there is gold; and the gold of that land is good: there is bdellium and the onyx stone. And the name of the second river is Gihon: the same is it that compasseth the whole land of Ethiopia. And the name of the third river is Hiddekel: that is it which goeth toward the east of Assyria. And the fourth river is Euphrates.
>
> Genesis 2:10–14, KJV

The first riverhead was *Pison*, which encompassed the entire land of Havilah where there was gold. The gold there was good, and there was bdellium and onyx stone. The name *Pison* means "flowing and increase,"[1] which implies fruitfulness, expansion and a constant flow of blessings and life. These waters wash away all barrenness, hopelessness, containment and unproductivity. These are healing waters that overthrow the thrones of iniquity and poverty. Notice there was gold in this flow, just as in my vision of the River of God. Gold represents not only the glory of God but also prosperity. So swimming in this part of the River frees us from all curses of lack and poverty.

The second head was *Gihon*, which means "a breaking forth."[2] Once again, the Breaker—Christ Jesus, who goes through the gates before us to ensure our full victory—breaks us out of containment and into our next measure of blessing and fulfillment. This flow of God's River breaks us out of our past and propels us into our future. No longer are we bound to Egypt and its death grip. When we flow in this part of the River, we are launched into our future Promised Land.

The third riverhead was named *Hiddekel*, which means "rapid and swift."[3] It also implies a swift horse, meaning that it is time to begin to run with the horses! When you swim in this part of the River, no longer are you at a slow brook; you have been released to run swiftly.

The fourth head of the river was named the *Euphrates*, which means "fertile and fruitful."[4] Once again, God confirms His desire for each of us to be blessed. He has given us the water of life. It is He who is the River of Life, and we can receive all these blessings if we are in relationship with Him.

> On the last and greatest day of the Feast, Jesus stood and said in a loud voice, "If anyone is thirsty, let him come to me and drink. Whoever believes in me, as the Scripture has said, streams of living water will flow from within him."
>
> John 7:37–38

We are created to live in a fruitful land and experience multiplication and expansion. In fact, it is a commandment to do so (see Genesis 1:28). As believers, we must fulfill our destinies and become fruitful. Being unfruitful is the opposite effect of our godly mandate. Jesus cursed the unfruitful fig tree (see Mark 11:14–20) not simply because He was hungry, but because that tree opposed the mandate from God that everything should be fruitful and multiply. God is judging every area of our lives that is unfruitful and commanding us to shift into fruitfulness and fulfillment.

Oh my goodness, did you get that? Any area of barrenness is being closely observed by the Lord. If you have received any prophetic words lately that have spoken to your barren situations, then, precious ones, God is expecting you to curse those barren areas and produce fruit! After Jesus cursed the barren fig tree, it withered up and died. We also need to curse every barren place so that the old passes away and we can experience God's new thing. Every person, every plant, every tree is commanded by God's law to increase.

All four of these riverheads are dependent upon a breakthrough stream that flows. The "Breaker" characteristic of God desires to go before you and break you out of a stagnant place of unfruitfulness.

Positioned at His Throne

The vision of the River that God gave me taught me that in order to flow in life, fruitfulness, increase and abundance, we not only have to flow in the River of God, but we also must remain properly positioned at the throne. If we are not before the throne, we easily can be in any river. To ensure that we are in only God's River, we must be before His throne, hear only His voice and experience only His instructions. Any river can flow and take us somewhere, but only God's River releases life and covenant breakthrough. Because the River of God flows from the throne, remaining consecrated before Him ensures that we are consistent with His flow.

In the vision, God and the River were One. He is the River! This is why it is so necessary to remain in the River—we need to remain in Him. And to remain in Him, we must be before His throne.

Some of you may be asking, "How can I remain before His throne?" First, you must realize that every challenge positions you to touch the hem of His garment. Many of us have been in the press—the position of desperation where we, like the woman with a twelve-year issue of blood, had to press in to touch God. When we get close enough to touch Him, we can easily see His face. In the River, we see His face (see Revelation 22:4), and we also swim in the healing waters. So, if you have been reaching out and touching the hem of His garment, then you also have been properly positioned to receive.

Also, in order to remain before the throne, you may need to enter a death season. By this I am referring to death to self and selfish ambition. Although we cry out for more of Him, it is often very difficult to remain steadfast with that determination. So we constantly must die to self. We will be positioned properly to experience a throne room ministry only if something dies.

In Isaiah 6, the prophet Isaiah was captivated with a vision of God's throne. Notice, however, that King Uzziah had to die before the prophet could see the Lord. In other words, old things, old relationships and old mindsets must die before we can truly see the King in all His glory.

In the year that King Uzziah died, I saw the Lord seated on a throne, high and exalted, and the train of his robe filled

the temple. Above him were seraphs, each with six wings:
With two wings they covered their faces, with two they
covered their feet, and with two they were flying.

Isaiah 6:1–2

The Narrow Place

We will not be able to swim in the River and experience the fullness of God's glory unless we are removed
from our past. This means we must be determined to de-
part from Egypt and cross over into the Promised Land.
The name *Egypt* means "black"[5] (indicating darkness),
"oppressors" (oppression) and "double straits" (double
narrow passages). Why would we want to continue to
go back to a dark place where we have been oppressed?
We are to walk in mantles of double-portion anointing,
yet we, like the Israelites in the wilderness, want to go
back into darkness just because we know what to expect
in that old place.

I am reminded of a baby in the birth canal, where it
is isolated and contained in darkness. Just at the time of
breakthrough and delivery, the baby experiences the narrow place. How uncomfortable to experience a narrow passage! How terrifying to face expansion when it has been
comfortable in the old place! Possibly the baby experiences
fear and terror as contractions push it into a constricted
atmosphere. I wonder how many babies would "go back"
if they could? It is possible that some have tried and caused
birth complications.

It is the very same with us. As we move into areas of
enlargement, we always face a narrow passage. The enemy
attempts to stop us at the gate of entry, and a demonic assignment works to keep us from swimming in the River
of Life.

The Python Spirit

One of the demonic forces that attempts to thwart our breakthroughs is the python spirit. When I first gained knowledge of the python spirit, I was going through a season of constant confusion. It was not just a one-day event; it was literally for weeks on end. I felt at times that I was losing my mind. On top of the confusion, I was battling fatigue, and no matter how much rest I took, it was never enough to regain my strength. I was also spiritually "stuck" and felt as if I could not break out into my place of increase. I prayed for days, and finally the Lord spoke to me in His "night voice" through a dream.

In my dream, a man was painting a picture. I stood in the distance watching the painter paint one layer of color upon another layer of color, and with each layer I could more easily "see" a picture of a witch. It was as if the witch had been hidden until the painter painted the picture, and as he finished, I could actually see what had once been hidden. Then the painter turned, looked me in the eye and said, "What was hidden from you is now revealed. The witch has placed a curse on you; it is a curse of divination."

I awoke from the dream completely unable to catch my breath. I experienced a choking sensation, as if someone were squeezing the life from me with a firm grip around my throat. Suddenly I heard the words *python spirit*. I knew it was the Lord speaking to me concerning the stronghold with which I was wrestling.

I was suddenly reminded of the apostle Paul when he addressed the spirit of divination in Acts 16:16. The Scripture unfolds the most interesting story of a woman who was traveling with Paul and Silas. At first she seemed to promote the men of God with flattering words about them. Yet at the same time, she was drawing more and more attention to herself. Paul properly discerned an evil spirit of divination, and he cast the evil spirit out of her.

Now it happened, as we went to prayer, that a certain slave girl possessed with a spirit of divination met us, who brought her masters much profit by fortune-telling. This girl followed Paul and us, and cried out, saying, "These men are the servants of the Most High God, who proclaim to us the way of salvation." And this she did for many days. But Paul, greatly annoyed, turned and said to the spirit, "I command you in the name of Jesus Christ to come out of her." And he came out that very hour.

Acts 16:16–18, NKJV

Did you notice that the Scripture said the girl with the spirit of divination was a "slave girl"? Isn't that interesting? The demon of divination is also known as "witchcraft," and it will make us its slave if we bow down to it. In other words, we can never allow entrance to a familiar spirit of witchcraft because the spirit will totally imprison us. This is the reason why God's Word instructs us not to open our lives to familiar spirits, soothsayers and the like (see Micah 5:12).

Divination is linked to the word *pythos*, which originates from the word *Putho*. Putho is the name of the region where the seat of a demonic oracle (someone who, under demonic influence, gave insight into situations) was located. In Greek mythology, the name of the Pythian (python) serpent or dragon that dwelt in the region of Pytho was said to have guarded the oracle at Delphi and been slain by Apollo.[6]

Let us return for a moment to the human birthing experience. When a child is birthed, it goes through a very narrow place in the birth canal, and the child must be "squeezed" tightly in order to be pushed through. Once it gets to the other side of its narrow challenge, its place of enlargement opens. In other words, the child goes through a "gated entrance," or a "threshold."

Spiritually, when a vision, ministry or opportunity is being birthed, there is also a narrow place of entrance before the enlargement. Just as the python snake squeezes the life and breath from its victims, the python spirit sits at the gate of entrance, the threshold of enlargement, and attempts to stop the birth by squeezing the breath from the vision. This is also the operation and strategy of the witchcraft spirit: to stop the vision or ministry from being fulfilled and enlarged.

One of the Hebrew words for *threshold* is *caph*,[7] which means "gate, door, post or threshold." It is from a root word meaning "to snatch away" or "to terminate." The second word used for *threshold* in the Hebrew is *pethen*, which means "to twist as a snake." This word is very close to the spelling and pronunciation of *python*. The snake in Scripture is linked with the occult, which is witchcraft. It is clear that as we go through any gate connected to our future, and as we pass through the threshold, there is a witchcraft "hold" on our future.

But there is hope! The King of Glory promises to go before us. He will go through the gates ahead of us to break us out of the old places and into our future.

> Lift up your heads, O you gates; be lifted up, you ancient doors, that the King of glory may come in. Who is this King of glory? The LORD strong and mighty, the LORD mighty in battle. Lift up your heads, O you gates; lift them up, you ancient doors, that the King of glory may come in. Who is he, this King of glory? The LORD Almighty—he is the King of glory.
>
> Psalm 24:7–10

Breaking Through into Enlargement

It is Christ, the Breaker, who leads the way through every gate of entrance; especially to our places of enlargement. Micah 2:13 says, "The one who breaks open will come up before them; they will break out [be birthed], pass through the gate, and go out by it; their king will pass before them, with the Lord at their head" (NKJV, my addition). In other words, the God of their future, Jehovah, led the way through every entrance, every gate, and broke them through every evil entanglement.

In her book, *The Breaker Anointing*, Barbara Yoder states:

> The Hebrew word for "break out" is *parats*. It means "to break out, burst out, to grow, to increase, to be opened." The implication is that something has been closed off, shut up, diminished, stunted, restricted or confined. . . . *Parats* has to do with breaking out of a prison-like structure, growing in something, increasing in any area, and opening that which has been shut up.[8]

She goes on to add: "In 1 Samuel 3:1 there is an example of breaking through. This passage is about the transition from an old system to a new one, or an old move to a new one."[9] Barbara Yoder refers to the times when the priesthood of Eli compromised and there was "no open vision (revelation)." The Hebrew word for "open" vision is *parats*, which basically is saying there was no breakout or breakthrough during the time of Eli's compromise.[10]

Dear ones, our destiny involves breaking through old religious paradigms and being thrust forth through every narrow place to embrace the new things of God. It is our birthing season; it is our season for open vision and breakouts from imprisonment. We can break out of the occult structure that keeps revelation "hidden" and in a dark place and break forth on the right and on the left into expansion and enlargement.

> Enlarge the place of your tent, and let them stretch out the curtains of your dwellings; do not spare; lengthen your cords, and strengthen your stakes. For you shall expand to

the right and to the left, and your descendants will inherit
the nations, and make the desolate cities inhabited.

Isaiah 54:2–3, NKJV

Clothe Yourself with the Warfare Mantle

In order to remain in the River and before God's throne,
we need two things. The first is a new warfare mantle that
empowers us with His might for spiritual battles ahead.
Don't assume that you will be able to remain in God's River
of Life without encountering demonic assault. The devil desires to kill us. He hates us because we are anointed! We must
clothe ourselves with God's mantle of authority because the
enemy has planned a death structure to defeat us.

The word *mantle* means "that which is thrown on or
around a physical covering" and refers to actual clothing,
such as a cloak or a robe.[11] A mantle is loose-fitting; this is
so that we may grow more fully into it.

God has new clothing for us! He has mantles that He
desires to release in this new season; it is time to change
our garments. We must take off the old and put on the new.
Moving from one level of glory to another requires growth
and maturity, thus fitting into the mantle of authority God
has given us.

The enemy will attempt to stop us, he will try to squeeze
life from us, and he will attempt to take our breath away.
But if we reach out and touch Jesus, brushing the hem of
His garment, He will heal us with His virtue, and we can
freely swim in His River.

Be Cleansed

The second thing needed to remain before His throne
is a fresh cleansing. The throne room is a holy place. The

angels are continuously crying, "Holy, holy, holy is the Lord of hosts."

Isaiah was caught up in a vision, observing God's glorious presence and the angels declaring God's holiness, when he noticed he was undone and unclean. He said, "Woe to me! . . . I am ruined! For I am a man of unclean lips, and I live among a people of unclean lips, and my eyes have seen the King, the LORD Almighty" (Isaiah 6:5).

In order for Isaiah to remain at the throne and witness God's glory, the angel had to touch his mouth and lips with a hot, fiery coal to cleanse him from his iniquity and sin. Only after the cleansing could Isaiah be sent out to fulfill his destiny.

It is the same with us. We must embrace seasons of cleansing and purity that will empower us to be sent forth, as Isaiah was, to fulfill our mission on this earth.

Embrace the Opportunity

The world *apostle* means "to be sent." During this season of apostolic sending forth, then, we will embrace more and more opportunities to receive the empowerment of the Holy Spirit by remaining in His River of Life and positioned at His throne. Although there is a price to be paid to remain properly positioned, it is so life-giving that we will be glad we endured the press!

Carefully read the blessing that is given when we overcome persecution: "To him who overcomes, I will give the right *to sit with me on my throne*, just as I overcame and sat down with my Father on his throne" (Revelation 3:21, emphasis mine).

Are you ready to position yourself at His throne? Position yourself now as you pray this prayer.

Father God, I desire to see Your glory. Like Moses, I seek Your face and I seek Your glory. I want to swim in Your River and experience the abundant life that comes only from knowing You and being in Your presence. I ask that You cleanse my heart from all unrighteousness and that You forgive me for my sins. I ask, Father, that You clothe me with a new mantle of holiness and a new armor for spiritual warfare so that I can remain in Your River. Although the enemy lies in wait at my gates of entrance, I am empowered to break through every threshold and defeat him. I trust You, Lord, with my entire future. Thank You for Your Word and for Your promises that declare I am victorious. In Jesus' mighty name, Amen.

Well, victorious ones, more *strategies from heaven's throne* await you. Let's move on!

10

CROSSING OVER INTO THE PROMISED LAND

"So I have come down to rescue them from the hand of the Egyptians and to bring them up out of that land into a good and spacious land, a land flowing with milk and honey."

Exodus 3:8

Moving forward is more than just finding the place called "There." The Lord brought His people out of captivity and provided a resting place for them, but they had to "cross over" to the other side in order to reap the harvest of their promises. The Lord also has provided a resting place for us. Crossing over into our land of promise, however, involves a deliberate act of obedience.

Sometimes the decision of the crossing is based on total submission to a prophetic destiny. But it is God's intention to bless our obedience that entices us to take the necessary steps toward the crossing.

Deuteronomy 28 describes the many blessings God gives us as the result of obedience:

> "If you fully obey the LORD your God and carefully follow all his commands I give you today, the LORD your God will set you high above all the nations on earth. All these blessings will come upon you and accompany you if you obey the LORD your God:
>
> You will be blessed in the city and blessed in the country.
>
> The fruit of your womb will be blessed, and the crops of your land and the young of your livestock—the calves of your herds and the lambs of your flocks.
>
> Your basket and your kneading trough will be blessed.
>
> You will be blessed when you come in and blessed when you go out.
>
> The LORD will grant that the enemies who rise up against you will be defeated before you. They will come at you from one direction but flee from you in seven.
>
> The LORD will send a blessing on your barns and on everything you put your hand to. The LORD your God will bless you in the land he is giving you."
>
> Deuteronomy 28:1–8

How can we possibly fail if we are obedient to the word of the Lord? The Lord is speaking to all of us in this season, directing us to embrace His new wine. He also has instructed each of us to leave the past behind, remove our old garments and put on a mantle of authority. We must embrace change.

God has good things planned for us! Aren't you excited? Victory has already been promised, and we will reap the harvest of many hidden treasures. An added blessing is to fully experience the land that flows with milk and honey.

What Does It Look Like?

Have you ever been on a blind date? My husband and I met on one. And I am so happy that I committed to that frightening experience! But what if I had backed away from the date because I had not seen the territory first?

Prior to a blind date, a picture would be nice, of course. But what if the person isn't photogenic and you judge by what you see in the natural? You could miss out on the best thing God has ever prepared for you! Committing to something so unknown and going on a date with someone you have not seen are like charging into a land that could be full of promises.

I am sure the Israelites wondered what the Promised Land looked like. At the time they were to enter, Joshua and Caleb were the only ones who had actually seen the land. The rest of the entire nation had to move forward on a promise. They knew they had to be obedient to go in and take the land, but they must have wondered what a land described as "a place flowing with milk and honey" looked like. They had no photographs to view, no *National Geographic* televised specials to entice them. They had to totally trust the Lord.

Oppressed and "Bent" by Iniquity

Trusting the Lord means first knowing His heart for us. The heart of God is to deliver us from the oppression of our old taskmasters. God has seen the affliction that "Egypt" has caused in our lives, and He has given us a supernatural charge to cross over into a land of freedom and promise: "The LORD said: 'I have surely seen the oppression of My people who are in Egypt, and have heard their cry because of their taskmasters, for I know their sorrows'" (Exodus 3:7, NKJV).

God said that He understood their sorrows. *Sorrows* translates as grief and pain, both physically and mentally. And as I previously stated, Egypt represents darkness, a doubly narrow place, and it symbolizes being oppressed by oppressors. The "oppressor," then, was the spirit behind Egypt. We identify "Egypt" today as "the world." We are to be in the world but not of (the spirit of) the world (see John 17:16).

The Scripture states the Lord had seen their "affliction." *Affliction* is a Hebrew word that is derived from a root word that also means "oppression," but in addition it means to "be bowed down, looking down, troubled, weakened, stooped over, humiliated (shamed) and in a weakened state."[1] Can you identify with any of these conditions? If you have felt oppressed by the spirit of Egypt and its Pharaoh (symbolic of a demonic stronghold), then I am sure the enemy has attempted to totally humiliate and weaken you so you can no longer look up. In fact, the enemy's plan is to keep us "stooped over and looking down" so that we cannot see where we are headed. After all, who can move forward into a future place of destination if he or she is looking at the ground?

The word *affliction* is linked closely to the word *iniquity*, which has several interesting connotations. It translates as "perverse, crooked, bowed down, to bend, twist and distort."[2] It is the devil's plan to distort our minds. He speaks lies, attempting to pervert God's Word so that we are unable to believe God's truths concerning our lives. We can become "bent" in our actions and thinking processes when the devil afflicts and persecutes us. During times of tests, trials and opposition from the enemy, the results are often patterns of "bent" thinking.

Very often, this pattern of bent thinking and bent behavior goes unnoticed. It becomes a part of our lifestyle, and it is even passed down through the generations. Like a tree limb that "bends" to work its way around an obstacle in its destined pathway so that it can find sunshine, we bend around obstacles and opposition. The subsequent iniquitous patterns stand in our way of full growth, thwarting us in our attempts to seek the Light. We are left with a permanent "bend" in our behavior and belief systems.

Iniquity, then, causes us to grow in the wrong direction. We tend to seek alternate paths and lifestyles rather than get delivered of the bent places. Maybe some of you have lived with bent patterns for so long that you have given up hope for deliverance—or you do not even know you need it. Remember that God heard the cries of the Israelites, His heart was moved toward them, and He delivered them from their oppression.

Steps to Crossing Over into Our Promised Land

Like the children of Israel, we have been oppressed by the spirit of darkness, and we have grieved and suffered shame, sorrow and weakness. But there is a way out! God sent us a deliverer—Jesus Christ! He has come to set us free from the oppressor. But we must do our part. Yes, dear ones, we have a part to play in our deliverance. Following are the steps we must take to cross over and take our Promised Land.

1. Put on the New Man

First we must examine our condition, which in turn determines our position. Ask yourself about your spiritual condition. What is your affliction? In what areas of thinking do you have a permanent "bend"? Do you suffer with doubt and unbelief? Do you trust God? These spiritual conditions will determine your position. Are you positioned to leave the past behind? Are you ready to remove yourself from the patterns of the old nature and put on the new man? It requires putting off the old man, which is corrupt, renewing your mind to the truth (believing what God states concerning you) and then putting on the new man. To become fully empowered to cross over and drive out your enemies, you must first properly position yourself and clothe yourself with the righteousness and holiness of Christ.

> That you put off, concerning your former conduct, the old man which grows corrupt according to the deceitful lusts, and be renewed in the spirit of your mind, and that you put on the new man which was created according to God, in true righteousness and holiness.
>
> Ephesians 4:22–24, NKJV

2. Decide to Cross Over

Now that you have determined to put on the new man, realize that the exit from the "old place" is to make a final decision to cross over to the other side. God really does have milk and honey waiting for you!

> "So I have come down to rescue them from the hand of the Egyptians and to bring them up out of that land into a good and spacious land, a land flowing with milk and honey—the home of the Canaanites, Hittites, Amorites, Perizzites, Hivites and Jebusites."
>
> Exodus 3:8

Crossing over to the other side is more than just crossing your Jordan. Although the Jordan is very significant in the process of possession, it is not limited to that one place of crossing. Like the Israelites and like Abraham, who faced several crossings as they pursued their promises, we, too, face numerous places that we must cross over. There is a Red Sea crossing, a crossing over from fear and anxiety to complete trust in God, a Jordan crossing, and many other crossings we face during our lifetimes.

3. Expect Miracles and Expansion

In Matthew 14:13, Jesus crossed the Sea of Galilee and then healed the sick. The Scripture actually says that Jesus was in a desert place, yet people traveled miles to witness His ministry, and with great compassion He healed them. In the evening, still in the desert place, Jesus fed the multitude with only five loaves and two fish. Wow! That must be what He meant when He said He would cause a river to flow in the wilderness and a path in the desert! We can expect the same miraculous manifestations when we begin to "cross over" to the other side.

Jesus crossed over the *Galilee*, which means "circuit, as enclosed, rolling and revolving."[3] This is similar to the word *cycle*, which means "a complete round or reoccurring series."[4] To cycle around something implies making a "circle," such as to go around and around in the same pattern. How many times have we circled and cycled around the same pattern of behavior? It is time to come out of an old cycle! When we come out (cycle out) of an old place and cross over into the new land, we experience expansion.

Jesus crossed over into greater expansion when He healed the sick and then when He blessed the meal, broke the bread and gave it to His disciples and the multitude (see Matthew 14:19). More than five thousand were fed and blessed due to Jesus' crossing over and cycling out from another place.

The very same thing can happen when we allow God to break us. Once we are broken, He can serve us to the Body of Christ, and we will witness great expansion.

4. Cross Over from the Other Side of Fear

Fear is one of the most powerful strongholds we face today. Fear causes insecurity, and insecurity produces unbelief. When fear is active, we see ourselves as small and ineffective rather than focusing on the majesty of God and believing that all things are possible. When we are ready to move forward into the future, the spirit of fear becomes very active against us, bringing fear and doubt and often causing paralysis.

Even Jesus' disciples had to cross over from the other side of fear. After feeding the multitudes, Jesus told the disciples to get into the boat and cross over to the other side again. Jesus went to the mountains to pray, but the disciples boarded the ship in an attempt to cross to the other side. Suddenly a storm came, and the disciples became fearful. Jesus walked out on the water toward them. The disciples thought Jesus was an evil spirit and were afraid. I believe a spirit of fear was sent to torment them because they began to doubt the word of the Lord.

When Jesus sends you to the other side, He has every intention of your making it! There is no reason to fear because His word to us is sure. When storms come in the crossing-over process, the devil uses the storm to cause us to fear and doubt the word of the Lord.

Jesus instructed the disciples not to be afraid. Only Peter responded with faith and walked on the water toward Jesus. When the winds became more boisterous, he began to fear again and then to sink. Jesus reached out, caught Peter and spoke to him: "You of little faith . . . why did you doubt?" (Matthew 14:31).

Isn't this exactly what occurs in our own lives? We receive a word from God to cross over into our land of abundance, so we get into our faith ship and make headway toward our promise. Then the devil comes, and he huffs and puffs and tries to blow down our house. If we respond with fear, we open the door to a spirit of torment.

Dear ones, when we get into this place, the only way out of fear is to get out of the boat and walk on the water in faith. The only other choice is to become paralyzed by fear and die in that ship. So let's get out of the boat and walk on some water! If we begin to sink, He will be there to stabilize us. He is with us, and we need to keep crossing over to get to the other side.

5. Remain Positioned before the Throne

In order to cross over into our promise, we must remain in the throne room. It is only here that we can meet God face-to-face. And only in the throne room can we position ourselves not only to see God, but also to hear His words and be led by Him into victory.

Isaiah faced the Lord after he left the "old" behind (see Isaiah 6:1). Isaiah could not move forward into his new season until he was properly positioned to see God's glory.

Moses was also a man to whom God spoke face-to-face. Moses saw God's glory and was determined never to move forward unless God's presence was with him. Unfortunately, Moses was unable to cross over and experience the land flowing with milk and honey. Although he was a man who experienced the miraculous, who saw God's glory and who was an appointed deliverer, Moses still missed it. Moses endured many tests in the wilderness, and because he took a wrong turn, he was not allowed to cross over into his promise. He used an old pattern based on how God had spoken in an old season, rather than listening to God's new word to him. Maybe he had developed a "bent" attitude. His mind-set hindered his entering into his promise.

6. Get Ready for a New Menu

There is a new food for us when we cross over. When the Israelites were in the wilderness, they were fed manna and quail. When they crossed over, however, the Lord changed their menu. They no longer received the nutrients from the old diet. In the Promised Land they were in the care of *El Shaddai*—the name for God that means the "all-sufficient, the many-breasted One, the nourishing, cuddling character of God." In the same way a baby depends totally on the mother's milk, the Israelites had to depend completely upon El Shaddai in the land of milk and honey.

In the new place the Israelites had to depend upon the fruit. It required more intimacy, more time in His presence for warfare strategy and more dependence on His leading than ever before. Israel had to remain properly positioned at all times to hear His instructions. Joshua had to remain close to God to hear His divine instructions concerning

- how to rise up, overcome fear and lead an entire nation across floodwaters (all within one chapter!);
- when to cross over the Jordan;
- where to camp before crossing;
- how to trust a harlot;
- where to cross;
- who was to cross over first;
- how many stones to take out of the Jordan to build a memorial;
- how to position the priests;
- what the priests were to do with their feet as they stepped into the Jordan;
- what to do with forty thousand people armed for war after they crossed over;
- when to stop and circumcise the males;
- how to actually convince the males that God said to circumcise themselves;
- how to shift from his paradigm concerning warfare and relate to the Captain of the Hosts!

It is the very same for each of us. As we cross over, we cannot be fed by words of the past. Whatever old patterns fed our behavior must be left on the other side of the crossing. As we move into our next place of promise, we are to receive nourishment from the promise. The promise is God's Word; all that He says about us, our circumstances and our condition must become our new diet. He is feeding us new bread. When we cross over, we are in His River of Life. It is time to shift out of the stinking thinking that has polluted our minds and blocked our breakthroughs!

7. Drive Out the Previous Tenants

Have you ever taken honey from a beehive? It requires war! If you want the fruit from "Beeland," you need a special strategy, and you must put on special military equipment to fight those devilish bees. They are fierce and very determined. They certainly understand the importance of unity; they swarm in mighty multitudes. One cannot even tell who the real leader is during an attack; they are all one and in one accord during their battles. They do not care who gets the medal of honor—they just want to kill!

The devil is not going to allow us to cross over into the Promised Land without a fight. Like the beekeeper taking honey from bees, we need a special strategy, and we must be equipped. We cannot go forward into our new place of milk and honey with old armor and old strategy. Old methods of warfare will not suffice, and just as in any war, new methods of warfare must be used. But first, we must understand who our enemies are and the strategies they use.

Thankfully, God gives us insight into our enemies and their tactics. In Exodus 3:8 the Lord said there were "-ites" in the land: Canaanites, Hittites, Amorites, Perrizites, Hivites and Jebusites. I visualize these -ites as demon-like termites that eat away at our foundations. Crossing over into the land of promise, then, requires warfare!

God said we are to "go in and possess the land." The word *possess* actually means that we are to take the land promised to us by driving out the previous tenants.

So before we cross over, we must position ourselves before the Father and seek Him for strategies of victory. King David put on the ephod and sought the Lord before battle. We also must seek the Lord for the strategies needed for this season.

Let's look closely at these enemies that block our growth. As you study the names of these -ites, see if you can recognize some of these strongholds in your own Promised Land. It might be possible that some have caused your bent behavior. In order to gain victory in your new place, you may have to remove yourself from the iniquitous pattern. You may have to kick out of your life the old, established tenants who have developed squatters' rights—the legal right to ownership someone receives simply because he/she has inhabited the land for a long period of time.

Canaanite

This name means "to be subdued and brought low." It literally means "to press down or humiliate."[5] We all can identify times when we have felt humiliated and pressed down or depressed. The anointing of God's Spirit can empower us to rise above our circumstances and defeat and conquer this enemy.

Hittite

This name means "an annoyer, annoyance, causing dread and fear."[6] Have you ever felt terrorized? Maybe you have suffered from anxiety or even had anxiety attacks that paralyze you. I often wonder how many of us miss out on the Promised Land because of fear. This stronghold caused the entire camp of Israel to miss its destiny! Fear is the direct opposite of faith. God mentions the words "Fear not" in the Scripture 365 times—once for every day of the year. We need not fear because He promises to send His presence before us into battle.

Amorite

This name means "a talker and a slayer,"[7] which implies a false voice speaking against us, an accuser or even a false prophecy. The enemy will falsely prophesy to you. He will speak exactly the opposite of what God has said concerning you and your future. We must discipline ourselves not to listen to his lies. We must be careful to set a watch over our speech, taking care not to speak negatively. We must not murmur and complain. Discipline your mind to think only on what is good, true, honest, just, pure, lovely and of a good report (see Philippians 4:8). Discipline yourself to renew your mind consistently; this will remove "bent" thinking.

Perrizite

This name means "a squatter, open and without walls."[8] It implies an unwalled city and a lack of self-discipline, which open a person's life to constant bombardment from the enemy. If we do not establish a watch over our speech, our thinking processes and our ears, then we will give the enemy squatter's rights in our lives. If we are consistent to discipline ourselves, however, then we will experience victory on a daily basis.

Hivite

This name means "declarer, pronouncer, one who lives, and is a villager."[9] It is similar to the name *Amorite*, but since it is a villager-type stronghold, it "lives" with us. I consider this stronghold a familiar spirit, which is a demonic spirit often assigned to us at birth.

The word *familiar* means "to be well acquainted with, closely intimate or personal, or pertaining to a family or household."[10] This spirit is like family, and over time we trust its voice. A familiar spirit gets so "familiar" that many times we do not recognize its influence upon our lives and thought patterns. It can speak to us easily, and we will not challenge its voice because it is such a familiar sound. This type of spirit is one of the most seductive and dangerous strongholds that attack us.

The witch of Endor, whom King Saul sought concerning his future, had a familiar spirit (see 1 Chronicles 10:13–14). In disobedience and rebellion, Saul removed himself from hearing God's voice. As a result of an ungodly "need to know," which, as I stated earlier, opens the door to witchcraft, he opened himself to ungodly counsel, and he died for his transgression. A familiar spirit is closely connected to a spirit of divination, so we must be careful to guard against the enemy, who falsely prophesies lies to us. Once again, by heeding only God's Word we can drive this -ite from our Promised Land.

Jebusite

This name means "to be polluted and trodden down."[11] This is another stronghold that implies depression and oppression. This name also implies defilement. King David conquered the Jebusites when he took the stronghold of Jebus and later renamed the city Jerusalem. *Jerusalem* means "double peace."[12] The enemy has robbed us of our peace and joy by oppressing us. Through Christ Jesus we have been given perfect peace. God's peace drives away all fear and anxiety, along with depression.

Israel had to conquer several other nations, as well. These are only a few that are mentioned in the Scripture, but these were the ones of which the Lord spoke directly.[13]

Remember that the Israelites did not conquer their enemies all in one day; the Lord drove them out little by little. So please be patient as you go into spiritual warfare and drive the enemy from your territory.

> The LORD your God will drive out those nations before you, little by little. You will not be allowed to eliminate them all at once, or the wild animals will multiply around you. But the LORD your God will deliver them over to you, throwing them into great confusion until they are destroyed.
>
> Deuteronomy 7:22–23

Realizing that God goes before us to defeat our enemies helps us to be more patient for our complete healing and deliverance. He is a faithful God, and He will perform all He has promised.

God Is the Promise

The land of milk and honey was a place of fullness and abundance. In fact, *milk* translates as "abundance" and refers to the fatness of the land. Its meaning even implies "bone marrow,"[14] which is the life-giving source to the bones.

Do you remember in chapter 5 when we studied the bones of Elijah and how the structure of Elijah resurrects what seems dead? Do you recall that fully housing God's presence requires a new structure? Well, our land of promise is the new structure. The promise is all that God is! He is the promise, and He is the land for which we long.

Dear ones, when we fully believe His Word, when we embrace all that He is and who we are in Him, then we are actively crossing over into our new season and we are possessing our new land. Although the Promised Land represents an actual spiritual place, we enter into that new land when we allow Him to be the structure of our lives, businesses, ministries and families. When we give Him full control, then we can possess every promise.

Steps to Take to Cross Over into the Promise

Are you ready to cross over into your Promised Land? Following these simple steps to freedom will place you on your pathway out of the wilderness. Speak these six areas, make a prophetic declaration, and then stand up and declare your freedom!

1. I renounce . . .

Take some time to renounce any area of unbelief, sin, addiction and false belief. Renounce any "bent" behavior or thinking. Look over the negative effects of the -ites and renounce any areas that relate to your life.

2. I acknowledge . . .

Acknowledge the truth. Begin to speak what God has declared concerning you. Some of you may desire to gather written prophecies and speak the prophetic words aloud to confirm God's perfect will. Acknowledge that Jesus died for your sins and that His blood cleanses you from all past iniquity.

3. I forgive . . .

Words and actions of others can cause deep wounds and rejection, which hinder our future. List the names, if possible, of those whom you need to forgive, including yourself. Remember to name spiritual authorities, teachers, governmental figures, etc.

4. I submit . . .

Submit to the plan of God for your life, to legitimate spiritual authority and to the Word of God.

5. I take responsibility . . .

Take responsibility for your choices in life. Then develop a disciplined lifestyle, and be determined to blame others no longer for your mistakes or for your situation.

6. I disown . . .

Make a decision to disown the sins of others, generational strongholds and your own sins. Place the sins on the cross and allow the blood of Jesus to cleanse you from your past.

The Power of a Prophetic Declaration

Declarations have tremendous power. Remembering that life and death are in the power of your tongue, make this prophetic declaration concerning your future:

I declare that I am moving past all generational sins and strongholds and that I remove myself from all "bent" behavior. I realize that God has a plan and a purpose for my life. He has a land of promise that awaits my possession, and I declare that no demon will stop me from taking my territory! I declare that no hindrance from my past will stop me from moving forward and fulfilling my destiny. I declare that God has provided a River in the desert and a way out of my wilderness. God has His very best planned for my life. Amen!

Now, precious ones, cross over into that land that is flowing with all of God's blessings. Press past every obstacle that attempts to stand in the way of your victory. You are in right standing with God. He has gone before you and defeated all of the -ites in your territory. The land is yours to take!

11

Seekers of His Glory

But when you pray, go away by yourself, shut the door
behind you, and pray to your Father in private. Then your
Father, who sees everything, will reward you.

Matthew 6:6, NLT

As you seek higher levels of God's glory, it becomes increasingly important to remain properly positioned and in His divine presence. Remaining properly positioned requires staying "hidden" in Christ. In this special, tucked-away place that is both private and intimate, He covers you with His wings and hides you unto Himself. As you dwell there, you develop a passion to understand the mysteries of God. When you seek Him in this hidden place, He promises to repay you. I believe that part of His reward is opening up to you realms of revelation and understanding. In the secret place, God reveals His secret plans and gives you His heavenly strategies to overcome the enemy.

The Ancient of Days desires to speak to each of us in the secret place and unveil the many mysteries from days past. He reveals ancient strongholds and hidden revelations needed for such a time as this.

> He who dwells in the *secret place* of the Most High shall abide *under the shadow* of the Almighty. I will say of the LORD, "He is *my refuge* and *my fortress*; my God, in Him I will trust." Surely He shall deliver you from the snare of the fowler and from the perilous pestilence. He shall *cover* you with His feathers, and *under His wings* you shall take refuge; His truth shall be your shield and buckler. You shall not be afraid of the terror by night, nor of the arrow that flies by day, nor of the pestilence that walks in darkness, nor of the destruction that lays waste at noonday. A thousand may fall at your side, and ten thousand at your right hand; but it shall not come near you. Only with your eyes shall you look, and see the reward of the wicked.
>
> Psalm 91:1–8, NKJV, emphasis mine

We, as believers, must remain hidden under His wings. In that "hiddenness," we are divinely protected from our enemies. But even more than that is the deliverance from the fear of any "false covering."

The Occult Spirit

An occult spirit attempts to "falsely cover" us with lies and deceit. The occult spirit's main purposes are to hide the truth, to lead us into deception and to seduce us to believe his lies. Let us examine the word *occult* in order to better understand how the enemy uses it to "cover" us in this way.

First, the word *occult* means "a system claiming to use knowledge of secret or supernatural powers."[1] Satan attempts to twist and distort the mysteries and secrets—the revelation—of God. Because the Body of Christ is receiving greater levels of revelation, we must be sure we are listening to the correct voice.

Another definition of *occult* is "secret, disclosed and hidden from view."[2] This implies that the enemy will keep revelation hidden from us. The word *revelation* means that something once "hidden" becomes "revealed." The words *occult* and *revelation* are closely connected, and we must be extremely discerning as we make advancements into deeper revelation. In other words, Satan schemes and places snares in front of us so that we will stumble, become confused and heed the wrong voice while uncovering mysteries. We are reminded that we are to seek the "mysteries" of God and not the "mysterious." The occult spirit tempts us with the "spooky and mysterious," and although at times God is mysterious, He protects His mysteries until He reveals them to His prophets.

One further definition of *occult* is "to block or shut off from view, to hide."[3] Again, the enemy's assignment is to block our view and keep the truth of God hidden from us. He blinds us with circumstances and mountains that seem to stand in our way. When challenged with demonic attacks, our minds become confused, our bodies become weak and we are unable to "see" our way.

Precious ones, the devil is a liar and a deceiver. He desires to hinder our ability to see properly and disable our ability to receive God's revelation. Satan also twists truth and distorts vision to get us to align with his lies, thus allowing his false covering to guide us.

Occult Spirits Try to Conceal Demonic Activity

Another purpose behind an occult spirit is to conceal and hide from exposure the demons blocking our breakthroughs. We are blinded to their activity and cannot determine the stronghold behind the situations. But God's Spirit of revelation—one of the sevenfold Spirits of God—reveals the demonic activity and gives us wisdom to battle these occult spirits.

One way occult spirits conceal demons that block our breakthroughs is to cover up the root causes of puzzling medical conditions. My husband, for example, battled kidney failure symptoms, fatigue and heart-related pain for months. Yet when he underwent a multitude of tests, his heart appeared to be perfectly normal, and no one could find the cause of his medical condition. My spiritual discernment spoke loudly that these physical ailments were manifestations of a serious heart condition. Finally we insisted on one more medical procedure, which demanded a hospital visit. I called our intercessors to pray against an occult spirit, which causes things to remain hidden and masked. We prayed and fasted for three days, and the next test revealed that he had three main blockages in his heart! He was immediately scheduled for open-heart surgery. He had the triple bypass heart surgery and is doing well today. But if it had not been for God exposing what was hidden, he might have died.

Thank the Lord for revelation!

The Hidden Things Can Cause Fear

As we embrace God's New Thing, He establishes a new order and government. But we often can be fearful of the New Thing. Fear can "cover" us, and conversely, we must be "covered" by God's Spirit in order to overcome this tool of the enemy.

When Moses died, the Lord told Joshua to rise up, cross over the Jordan and lead the people:

> After the death of Moses the servant of the LORD, it came to pass that the LORD spoke to Joshua the son of Nun, Moses' assistant, saying: "Moses My servant is dead. Now there-

fore, arise, go over this Jordan, you and all this people, to
the land which I am giving to them—the children of Israel.
Every place that the sole of your foot will tread upon I have
given you, as I said to Moses. From the wilderness and this
Lebanon as far as the great river, the River Euphrates, all the
land of the Hittites, and to the Great Sea toward the going
down of the sun, shall be your territory."

Joshua 1:1–4, NKJV

Once again, the old had to die in order for the Lord's
plans and purposes to be seen. Moses—the old order—was
dead, and now a new plan and a new order was being established. Joshua was instructed to leave the past behind
and embrace the new challenge of moving forward.

But Joshua faced fears as he stepped up to the plate. He
was told by the Lord three times to be strong and of good
courage and not to fear: "Have I not commanded you? Be
strong and courageous. Do not be terrified; do not be discouraged, for the LORD your God will be with you wherever
you go" (Joshua 1:9). The Lord told Joshua that there was
no need to fear his future or the giants in the land because
He would be with him in the journey.

Like Joshua, every one of us faces fear when moving out
of what has been familiar into the unknown. What is "hidden" from us can overshadow us with great fear. But God
is with us. He does not desert us. "He guides me in paths
of righteousness for his name's sake" (Psalm 23:3).

Joshua is an example of how to remain properly aligned
with God's purposes, especially during seasons of change
and transition. He pressed through any possible fear and
intimidation. He remained obedient as he led God's army
across the Jordan and into unfamiliar territory. Although
there were many giants in the land of promise, Joshua remained stable and full of faith. He allowed God's Spirit to
cover him so that the spirit of fear could not, and he subse-
quently led God's army into a season of possession.

King Saul's Disobedience and Fear

In contrast to the powerful, faithful example of Joshua stands King Saul—a prime example of a self-centered, disobedient leader. Saul felt he had a "better way" than God and forfeited his destiny because he rejected the Lord. Whereas Joshua led God's army into a season of possession, Saul led his army into a season of regression and spiritual depression. Joshua led the Israelites forward into their future; Saul led them backward because of his own disobedience. Joshua's leadership was a catalyst of resolve and resolution; Saul's leadership was tainted with selfishness, fear and rebellion.

Under Saul's leadership, the Israelites began to fear their enemies. Instead of facing the Philistines, they ran and hid among rocks, caves and thickets. Can you imagine? The Israelites were on a roll. They had been favored by God in battle and had collected the spoils. But suddenly a spirit of fear overtook their faith.

Fear is the opposite of faith. Remember: The occult spirit promotes a demonic force of "hiddenness." If we fear, then the enemy attempts to overshadow us with torment and cause us to respond with a need to become "hidden" or to "run and hide in fear." As a result, we easily open doors for other occult spirits to occupy our minds and we make ourselves open to the enemy's lies and deception. Fear, then, causes us to hide and prevents us from moving into the next level of God's glory.

Let's not be like Saul and the Israelites and "hide" from our enemies. God says, "The one who is in you is greater than the one who is in the world" (1 John 4:4). We must be on guard as we move forward and gain new territory, having faith in His power to overcome rather than succumbing to fear that our own power will not be enough. Only in this way will God's glory be more fully manifest in us.

Don't Hide from God; Hide in Him

Because we are shifting out of an old paradigm that exposes belief systems, it will shake our personal "government." What has governed our lives in the past will be shaken so that God can establish a new order in our lives. The Lord desires to be the One who orders our steps and, therefore, ensures our victory. His plans are to release us to a new measure of victory and authority. Let's study more closely what happened to King Saul so that we can understand how to shift out of the old and establish the "new" in our lives.

As 1 Samuel 13 begins, Saul had reigned for two years over Israel and then chose three thousand men to battle the Philistines. He was about to lead Israel into battle, but Saul failed the test when he was measured by God.

In Saul's army were three thousand men. Two thousand were in the city of *Michmash* (meaning "hidden"[4]) at Bethel, and another thousand were with Jonathan in *Gibeah* (meaning "high place"[5]) of Benjamin. The names of these places offer spiritual insight into both positive and negative attributes of the people of God. Eventually the people were called together in *Gilgal* (meaning "a wheel rolling, indicating cycling"[6]).

Positively we could say that God's children were in a "high place" in God, seated in heavenly places and "hidden" away in His secret place with divine protection. From such a place, they could "cycle" out of any wilderness mentality, fears of failure and defeat and rise above their circumstances (to a "high place") to defeat their enemy. This is how the Israelites should have seen themselves.

But negatively, the Israelites, led by Saul, chose to be defiled in their thought processes. Rather than focusing on the positive attributes of God's ability to fight on their behalf, they focused on the fact that the Philistines had thirty thousand chariots, six thousand horsemen and as many people as the number of the sands. Talk about feeling overwhelmed by the odds!

Remember, the name *Philistine* means "to wallow in the mud"[7] and represents defilement. Battling against the Philistines defiled the Israelites' faith and determination. The occult stronghold grasped hold, and they chose not to remain "hidden in God," but instead ran and became "hidden":

> When the men of Israel saw that they were in a strait, (for the people were distressed,) then the people did hide themselves in *caves*, and in *thickets*, and in *rocks*, and in *high places*, and in *pits*.
>
> 1 Samuel 13:6, KJV, emphasis mine

Have you ever run and hidden? Maybe you have found yourself hiding in a cave before. The enemy attempts to make us run to places that may appear safe but are really places of great danger because occult spirits have established strongholds over those "hiding places." Remember: The occult spirit is determined to attach a false authority and false covering over us that will speak lies and wear us down. Its main assignment is to wear us down so that we finally break down and make covenant agreement with the lies.

These places of the Israelites' hiding also give us spiritual insight into the snares of the enemy. The word *cave* means "naked and ashamed."[8] If we run to a cave, we will end up completely vulnerable to the enemy. Isolation in a cave experience is very dangerous. We must remain connected to the Body of Christ and remain accountable to spiritual authority. To separate from accountability is to become totally vulnerable to deception.

Another place the Israelites hid was in a thicket. One of the translations of the word *thicket* means "hook."[9] The enemy desires to hook us to the past. The enemy wants to chain us to our past responses of fear, doubt and unbelief.

Rocks represent anything in our lives that is a foundation other than Christ. Jesus is the only Rock, and any other foundation is shaky ground. We cannot depend upon any natural foundation, such as money, possessions or relationships. Jesus Christ is our only sure foundation.

One of the translations of the word for *high places* means "cliffs" and is rooted in the words *battle cry* and *roar*.[10] Do you know that the enemy has a false roar? When a lion's pride is left alone while the male hunts for food, there is the threat of another lion entering the camp. A false authority can enter into the camp and roar over them. Yet it is a false roar—one not given from the lion in true authority. The lion's pride must be well-trained to hear and discern the true roar. In turn, we also must be careful that we do not run to hide within a false roar. A false roar would be a false sense of security—maybe the security of a past relationship or a past belief system. Dear ones, it is time to let go of old security blankets and follow only the roar of the Lion of Judah!

The word *pit* means "dungeon and prison."[11] If we run and hide anywhere other than God, we become open prey to a demonic lockdown. If we remain in an old, defiled place, we will remain in a spiritual prison. Jesus Christ has come to set us free! There is a way out from the old thing. He has made a way for us—a way in the wilderness and a river in the desert. We must run to His secret place.

Elijah Had to Come Out of the Cave for His New Assignment

Elijah also hid in a cave. But there was much more for Elijah to do for the Kingdom of God.

When it was time for Elijah to go out on a new assignment, he had to come out of the cave, go back, anoint a new leader and mentor Elisha. When Elijah obeyed and shifted out of hiding, an entirely new structure was developed. A new government was established when he anointed Jehu, who later destroyed Jezebel, the false occultic authority over Israel. Elijah also called Elisha to the role of prophet and imparted to him a double-portion anointing.

You, too, have great things to do for God. If you are hiding in an old place, come out! Leave your place of hiding and hide yourself in God. Position yourself before His throne and gain fresh strategy as you cross over into fullness. It is time to speak to whatever stands in your way, so that it can be removed. You are destined for greatness!

God's System of Measurement

I said earlier that Saul failed when God measured him. Saul had three thousand men—the number three multiplied by one thousand. "Thousand" represents ten multiplied by the number one hundred. Biblically, "ten" represents a "measurement"—usually for the purpose of accepting or rejecting. Any time there is a number multiplied by ten, it can be considered a measurement of acceptance or rejection. In other words, when God measures (symbolized by multiples of ten), it is for His purpose of accepting or rejecting what He has measured.

Let me give you an example. When Israel was in the wilderness for forty years, the number for this season was four years multiplied by ten. This indicates a measurement on God's part. Four is the number for the natural creation, circumstances and surroundings. While the Israelites were in the wilderness, they continually faced challenges that involved their natural needs, such as the daily provision of water and food. Their natural surroundings were the desert, in which there was no water. God used their natural surroundings to measure—test—them.

Well, just one day without food is enough to bring on an irritable attitude, so I can't even begin to imagine how difficult it was to have faith for food and water in the desert. The Israelites' response was not good; they were fearful, hungry, thirsty and weary. They began to murmur and complain. God was so angry with their response that He was tempted to destroy them many times. In fact, all but two of the complainers died in the wilderness and never saw their promise. But God's period of testing and measurement worked. At the end of the forty years, God "measured" them. What He saw was a new generation of great potential. They measured up! So He then empowered Joshua and a new group of warriors to cross over.

If God were to measure you right now, what would He calculate? Would He say that you were complacent? Would He say that you were compromising? Would He say that you did not want to let go of your past and move forward?

When I was a child, my mother would get out her yardstick and "measure" my growth. I will bet you had marks on your wall, too! It is an exciting thing when we grow up to look back at those marks and see how we have grown.

God wants us to be blessed by His measuring. He wants us to look back and see how we have grown. And He wants to give us more of His glory. God is measuring our maturity right now because He wants to bless us with more of His glory and presence.

Measuring the Waters in the Sanctuary

Let me ask you another question—a very serious one: How deep do you really want to go in God?

The Word says, "Deep calleth unto deep at the noise of thy waterspouts" (Psalm 42:7, KJV). A waterspout is a whirling, funnel-shaped cloud that touches the surface of a body of water. It is a duct that discharges large amounts of water. Spiritually speaking, God's waterspouts are mighty winds of God—supernatural whirlwinds—that appear and create a portal of His glory. They are symbolic of God's presence, power and glory. His waterspouts release a watering of His Spirit, which begins to fill the temple with His presence.

I believe God is measuring our temples to determine how much of His glory we desire. Will we settle for a measurement where only ankle-deep waters are released?

> Then he brought me back to the door of the temple; and there was water, flowing from under the threshold of the temple toward the east, for the front of the temple faced east; the water was flowing from under the right side of the temple, south of the altar. He brought me out by way of the north gate, and led me around on the outside to the outer gateway that faces east; and there was water, running out on the right side. And when the man went out to the east with the line in his hand, he measured one thousand cubits, and he brought me through the waters; the water came up to my ankles. Again he measured *one thousand* and brought me through the waters.
>
> Ezekiel 47:1–4, NKJV, emphasis mine

The river in this passage of Ezekiel represents God's glory. The first measurement, one thousand cubits, was a level for those who settle for being "ankle deep" in God's Spirit. One thousand cubits equals ten (measurement to accept or reject where we are in the Spirit) multiplied by one hundred, a number that represents fullness, full measure and full reward. God is determining if we are ready for a "full" measure and a "full reward."

The number one thousand also represents maturity. When God measures our temple, He measures with one thousand cubits of increase. In other words, He moves us from one level of maturity to the next level of maturity. In Ezekiel 47, every new level of the river was measured in one thousand cubits!

Verses 4 and 5 show that with each increase of one thousand cubits, the level rises, first to the knees and then to the waist:

> Again he measured one thousand and brought me through the waters; the water came up to my knees. Again he measured one thousand and brought me through; the water came up to my waist.
>
> Ezekiel 47:4, NKJV

And then look at verse 5 (NKJV):

> Again he measured one thousand, and it was a river that I could not cross; for the water was too deep, water in which one must swim, a river that could not be crossed.

Now these waters were so deep, it was a river to swim in. These are the same waters of the River of God that flow from the throne—the River in which we have been seeking to swim. It is a river of life, healing and glory!

> When I arrived there, I saw a great number of trees on each side of the river. He said to me, "This water flows toward the eastern region and goes down into the Arabah, where it enters the Sea. When it empties into the Sea, the water there becomes fresh. Swarms of living creatures will live wherever the river flows. There will be large numbers of fish, because this water flows there and makes the salt water fresh; so where the river flows everything will live.
>
> Ezekiel 47:7–9

The Lord is measuring us to determine how much of His glory we truly desire. Are you ready to make your shift and jump into God's River? Being in His secret place empowers you to remain positioned for your entrance into His glory. You are being empowered to move from one level of glory to another level of glory. Do not fear your future! Simply trust His leading because He is covering you with His shadow of protection.

The Pool of Siloam

> Having said this, he spit on the ground, made some mud with the saliva, and put it on [anointed] the man's eyes. "Go," he told him, "wash in the Pool of Siloam" (this word means Sent). So the man went and washed, and came home seeing.
>
> John 9:6–7

The Pool of Siloam ("sent") was a watering place. After Jesus anointed a blind man's eyes with clay, He then "sent" the man to wash in the Pool of Siloam. The man obeyed. He washed and came back with his sight fully restored.

Originally, the pool was meant only for the inhabitants of Jerusalem. The workers had constructed a tunnel to route the waters inside the city walls and empty into a pool-reservoir. This tunneling brought waters inside the city walls and denied access to these waters to invaders of Jerusalem. So these waters were a "secret place" and "hidden" from the enemy.

God has secret, hidden waters for each of us. As we swim in His waters we experience healing and restoration.

Today in Israel, there is much excavation at the site of the Pool of Siloam. In fact, this "healing pool" is even being restored. This physical reality is a spiritual sign that the waters of God are still active and alive. His flowing waters are restoring the hope of healing and restoration!

Refresh yourself in God's healing waters—His place of sending. Allow the Lord to speak to you in His secret place concerning the places He desires to send you. Maybe it is to minister to your family, in your place of employment, in your circle of friends. Maybe God is calling you to the nations. But wherever you are being sent, allow Him to send you in His time, and be sent with His blessing and authority. When you do so, the measures of God's glory being manifested in your life will increase immeasurably.

12

Establishing Your
Victory Structure

In [Him] the whole building, being fitted together, grows
into a holy temple in the Lord, in whom you also are being
built together for a dwelling place of God in the Spirit.

Ephesians 2:21–22, NKJV

"It's beautiful! I love the design! This is going to be a gorgeous house. The layout of each room is perfect. The kitchen has a wonderful flow pattern for traffic. The family room is spacious. It is just perfect!" I was observing a set of construction plans. My husband and I were building our very first home, and I was elated.

I know that to many of you building a house is not important, but I have been exposed to the home-building business since I was a teenager. My parents were successful homebuilders for over forty years, and I grew up smelling sawdust on the job. It was my dream to build a home!

After our final approval of the construction plans, the foundation was prepared and poured—solid concrete for that needed stability. The foundation, when finished, did not look like much at all—just a sheet of solid grey. But I was aware that the foundation was very important because the entire house would be built upon that grey mixture of rocks and other materials.

I was ready for the next stage—the framing—so that I could actually see something happening. I looked forward to the lumber shaping every wall, beam and roofline.

The framers came early, and by the time I arrived, several walls were up. *How exciting!* I said to myself. *Walls!* I remained on the jobsite for hours watching the framing crew erect the walls. They chalked off every room, measured the lumber, sawed each piece and then—rooms! Several days later the framing was completed, the roof was on, and we began the interior work on the home.

Although I love decorating a home, the framing part of building is still my favorite. I am very aware how important "framework" is; it totally shapes a home. The framework is the structure that holds a house together.

The process of building a home can be compared to the process of building our spiritual lives. How are our spiritual homes built? Most of the time we focus on the foundation—and rightly so. Our spiritual houses need to be built upon the solid Rock of Christ Jesus. But we also need to look closely at our framework and examine what has framed our lives (see Luke 6:48).

What Is Our Framework?

If we were to take a snapshot of our lives today and place that photograph within a frame, we would be able to determine what had framed our world. How would that framework differ from our hopes and dreams? In other words, what failures, setbacks and life cycles have hindered our dreams from being within that framework?

Many of us still live in the past, which is the reason our past is still in the framework, or structure, of our lives. Ask yourself: "What does my structure consist of?" Are you experiencing the fullness that you desire? Are you experiencing the victory God promised? Do your prophetic words declare breakthroughs that you have not experienced? If you have answered no to any of these questions, then it is time for you to shift from an ungodly structure of defeat into God's victory structure. It is time for you to go before God and receive fresh strategies from His throne for your life.

Bringing the Unseen into Existence

God framed the world with His words. He sees everything from a state of completion. At the time of creation, He framed the entire universe with invisible words (see Hebrews 11:3). At the very instant we were created in our mothers' wombs, He formed and fashioned us after His own image. God had a plan, a structure, a framework that He spoke into existence. His plan was a picture of our future that was framed in heaven.

But the enemy came into our lives and sowed his demonic seeds of lies and deceit into our hearts. As a result, our belief systems became defiled, and we developed religious paradigms that limit God and His ability to heal and restore us. Rather than believe that we are chosen, loved and accepted, we believe that we are abandoned, rejected and unloved. As a result of our pain, we have made many wrong choices, and our lives are framed with hopelessness and despair.

God's desire is to restore us and empower us to fulfill our destiny. He wants each of us to know that He has not abandoned or forsaken us and that He is the Great Physician and the Great Restorer of hopes and dreams. The prophet Joel declared, "I will restore to you the years that the swarming

locust has eaten" (Joel 2:25, NKJV). It is God's heart's desire
to restore all that has been destroyed by the enemy.

God desires to bring the unseen into existence. When He
created the universe, it was unseen and then became visible. As
He restructures your life, the very same will happen for you.

> Fear not, O land; be glad and rejoice, for the LORD has done
> marvelous things! Do not be afraid, you beasts of the field; for
> the open pastures are springing up, and the tree bears its fruit;
> the fig tree and the vine yield their strength. Be glad then, you
> children of Zion, and rejoice in the LORD your God; for He has
> given you the former rain faithfully, and He will cause the rain
> to come down for you—the former rain, and the latter rain
> in the first month. The threshing floors shall be full of wheat,
> and the vats shall overflow with new wine and oil.
>
> Joel 2:21–24, NKJV

The prophet Joel is declaring a new structure of victory.
God will release the latter rain and the spring rain together
in the very same month, meaning that you will experience
the flood of His power and anointing to break yokes. He is
going to overflow your life with the new wine, and your
barns will be full.

We cannot see this with our natural eyes; we must look
to our future with supernatural vision. If we are created
in God's image, we also can speak to the invisible and
declare it to become visible. We can frame our world with
words that God has declared and, therefore, experience a
new structure of victory. Don't let your enemy rob you of
shifting into your new victory structure!

Victory Structure #1: Ask God to Overshadow You with His Presence

We must know our season for enlargement and then
submit to that season. Remember when Mary, the mother

of Jesus, received the prophecy that she would become pregnant with Jesus? She was overshadowed by the Lord's presence and later birthed the prophetic declaration given to her by the angel Gabriel (see Luke 1:26–35). Mary's response to the word of the Lord was, "May it be to me as you have said" (Luke 1:38). She was quick to come into full agreement with the will of God and then experienced her season of enlargement (pregnancy). Mary not only fulfilled her destiny, but she gave birth to the destiny of another!

The very same potential is within each of us—to receive our prophetic destiny, become enlarged and pregnant with God's will and then give birth not only to our future but also to the future of the Kingdom. As we come into full agreement with God's Word, He will overshadow us with His presence and release us into our season of enlargement.

Let's not be like Zacharias, who doubted Elizabeth's ability to overcome her barrenness. Do you remember what happened to him? He was struck with dumbness so that he could not speak negatively. His negative confessions might have aborted God's plans, so the Lord made him unable to speak out against His divine will.

Although Elizabeth had been cursed with barrenness, God desired to bless her womb. The Lord also desires to bless us and our spiritual wombs. It is His desire to release us from all barrenness and desolation and to speak life into dormant dreams and destiny.

A Time Such As This: Overshadowed with Divine Destiny!

Let's take a look at the story of Esther. When her people were being threatened with extinction, Mordecai appealed to Esther and reminded her of the Jewish destiny concerning deliverance and enlargement. Mordecai said that deliverance and enlargement was destined to come, but unless Esther stepped into her place, neither she nor her descendants would witness the enlargement. Esther must have

realized that her moment to make a difference in history
had arrived. Although she most likely had not planned
for her life to take this particular charted direction, Esther
must have realized the potential for aborted destiny. As a
result, Esther applied faith to the favor granted her, laid
down her life and approached the king.

When Esther approached the king's throne, the curse of
death and destruction from Haman, the Amalekite, was
revoked. Esther and Mordecai then wrote a written decree
that every generation would remember:

> These days should be remembered and observed in every
> generation by every family, and in every province and in
> every city. And these days of Purim should never cease to
> be celebrated by the Jews, nor should the memory of them
> die out among their descendants.
>
> Esther 9:28

This season of remembrance established by Esther and
Mordecai was named Purim. The Feast of Purim is cel-
ebrated each year in the months of March and April, which,
in Hebrew terms, is referred to as Adar. The word *Adar*
means "the pregnant month,"[1] a spiritual time to conceive
the plans and purposes of God. Although we as Christians
are not legalistic in celebrating all the Jewish feasts, there is
great spiritual significance as to the reason for the feasts.

The Feast of Purim reminds us that we are in a season
when our spiritual womb is being prepared for enlargement. A supernatural pregnancy involves the Lord over-
shadowing each of us with His glory. Like Esther, we must
have faith that God has given us abundant favor and then
begin to walk in that new measure of godly favor.

Two Death Structures Threaten Enlargement

Esther knew that there were two death structures against
which she would be at war. One was the fear of death. Es-

ther knew that if the king had not summoned her and she initiated being in his presence, she could lose her life. The penalty for presumptuously approaching the throne was immediate death. Esther literally laid down her life for the destiny of the kingdom.

The second death structure was already in the making. It was a literal structure—the gallows—with a hangman's noose awaiting. Haman ordered the construction of the gallows specifically to hang Mordecai.

Precious saints of God, the enemy has also plotted against each of us. He eagerly awaits our destruction! The same two death structures await us today, spiritually speaking. Our enemy uses the Amalekite stronghold to abort destiny and bring us spiritual death. In my recent book, *Destiny Thieves*, I wrote several chapters on the Amalekite spirit and how this evil strongman aborts destiny.

But if we choose to die to self and embrace the advancement of the Kingdom of God, as Esther did, we can be empowered to walk in our full potential and achieve our destiny—and the Kingdom of God will be advanced! In order to fully cross over into our future, our Promised Land, we must defeat the Amalekite spirit.

Victory Strategy #2: Defeat and Overthrow Death Structures

Esther defeated the death structures not only by laying down her life for the benefit of the Kingdom, but also through divine favor. This awesome level of favor was given to Esther because of her character. Esther had endured twelve months of sacrifice and purification before she was allowed to approach King Ahasuerus. Twelve is the symbolic number of government. As a result of her dedication to purity, she was empowered to walk into a governmental position in which she was given power to reverse a decree of death against her, her household and the entire Jewish nation.

As modern-day Esthers, we, too, must endure a period of separation. If we also lay down our lives, develop the Kingdom mentality and allow the Lord to purify our motives, then it is possible that the same ability to reverse decrees of death will be given to each of us. We must pray over our prophetic words and promises and do warfare. We must obtain favor with the King through separation unto Him, obedience and laying down our lives.

As part of her purification, Esther bathed in myrrh for six months. Myrrh is bitter to the taste but has many healing qualities. To receive divine empowerment to overthrow death structures, we cannot skip the myrrh season. It will not be over in just one day, but we must endure the bitter experiences, allowing the Lord to heal our hearts and settle us firmly into His divine plans.

Myrrh was also an oil used to prepare bodies for burial. Once more, we recognize how valuable it is to die to self and selfish ambition in order to gain godly power and authority on this earth.

Esther's Hebrew name was *Hadassah,* meaning "myrtle."[2] The myrtle was an evergreen tree and its leaves, flowers and berries were used as perfume. Her name represents the beauty and fragrance we must also carry with us as we approach the King to gain favor. As a result, we, too, will be able to shift demonic structures of death and release life to our circumstances.

Victory Structure #3: Seek the King and His Kingdom

After her time of separation, Esther obtained favor to approach the king with her requests. Although it required a full twelve months to become properly positioned to approach the throne, it empowered her to later shift an entire government.

Esther changed her culture by paying the price that was required to remain in the throne room. She did whatever it took to seek the king and his kingdom. Esther's faith and gained favor resulted in an entirely new structure for her people. The Jewish people shifted from a death structure into a structure of blessing and expansion.

To shift out of an old religious paradigm and belief system we must realize that "it is no longer about us; it's about Him." Our plans for our future must include His plans for our future; in fact, His plans must become priority. We must go into the throne room and seek His heavenly strategies for our lives. If we, like Esther, are determined to lay down our own agendas and seek the King, then we can shift out of an old structure of bondage into a structure of victory.

Esther's time of separation prepared her for the future and allowed her to change the decrees of Haman, the Amalekite. The Amalekites were notorious for preying on the weak and feeble. They would lie in wait behind the moving camps and "pick off" the weak ones who lagged behind. Those who moved slowly were either murdered or robbed and taken into slavery. We cannot be slow in moving forward. We must decide today to follow God's leading. Don't remain behind when God is moving you from an old structure; shift today! Your determination to follow God's cloud of glory will empower you to develop a structure of victory and expansion. Seek Him and His Kingdom. Your faithfulness to remain in His Secret Place before the throne and to continue to seek His heavenly strategies will keep you in the River of Life.

Seek Him, and you will find Him. If you knock at heaven's door, He promises that heaven will open unto you. You cannot experience heaven without receiving His promises. God will extend His scepter to you, just as King Ahaseurus did to Queen Esther when he received her. It is time to step into your rightful position to shift your culture and establish a godly spiritual climate that will ensure your future victory.

Victory Structure #4: Decree a Thing and It Shall Be Established

Thou shalt also decree a thing, and it shall be established unto thee: and the light shall shine upon thy ways.

Job 22:28, KJV

When we make a decree, the Word of God says it becomes established. In other words, the decree can become a foundation upon which to build. Many of us are attempting to build our future, but we are not coming into agreement with God's Word. Therefore, we also are not decreeing what God has already spoken concerning the situation.

Satan has already devised a plan of destruction against us. Many of us have battled the spirit of death and aborted dreams since the time of our births. We can reverse every decree the enemy has made concerning our lives, however, by writing a new decree.

Esther wrote a new decree, and it released the entire Jewish nation from a death assignment:

King [Ahasuerus] replied to Queen Esther and to Mordecai the Jew, "Because Haman attacked the Jews, I have given his estate to Esther, and they have hanged him on the gallows. Now write another decree in the king's name in behalf of the Jews as seems best to you, and seal it with the king's signet ring—for no document written in the king's name and sealed with his ring can be revoked."

Esther 8:7–8

We also can write a new decree, which will reverse the curse of death. Just like Esther, God is giving us the same opportunities to write a decree concerning our finances, health, children, houses or whatever concerns us. We can reverse the enemy's old decrees that have framed our world and write a new decree, and God will seal it.

Pray, Get God's Direction, Write the New Decree

Dear ones, I encourage you to take some time to pray and write a decree. Get real with God. Getting up close and personal with the Father will ensure that your decree is from a pure motive. Pour out your heart to Him, and let His Spirit guide you while you write a new decree over your life. Then believe God to reverse the curse of death in every area of your life.

Here is an example of a written decree. (Remember: This needs to be in your own words.)

Father, I realize the devil has decreed death and destruction over my life. I have battled with a spirit of poverty and hopelessness for a very long time. I believe it began from the time I was born. Since I was a child, I have battled fear and anxiety. I realize that this is not what You have decreed over my life. You have stated in Your Word that I am called and chosen. Your Word states that I am the head and not the tail. I receive a new measure of faith today. I decree that I will no longer be fearful because I am trusting in You. In the name of Jesus, I repent from being in covenant with the words of Satan, and I believe that I am loosed from captivity. I am being established and positioned for abundant wealth according to Your divine purpose. In Jesus' name, Amen.

When Jesus was in the wilderness and Satan tempted Him, Jesus replied to His enemy with these words: "It is written." Now that you have written your decree that reverses the curse of death and destruction, tell the devil, "It is written," and shift into your new measure of victory.

Cross Over into God's Framework

For a very long season we have been experiencing God's *chronos* time—the natural time, the daily "grind" of life. In *chronos* time, we go through our normal daily activities, believing and hoping for the *kairos* time—the exact moment when a supernatural shift will occur and we will be launched into our promise.

Well, dear ones, this is the season for you to shift into your next season of possession. It is your time to enter God's throne room and see His heavenly strategies for your life. It is your time to plunder the enemy's camp and take back all that was stolen. It is time for your promise of breakthrough and blessing in every area to be unveiled.

Many of us still live in the past, which is the reason our past is still in the framework, or structure, of our lives. It is very important for each of us to realize that we are in a *kairos* time now. We must do what it takes to shift out of ungodly structures of defeat into God's victory structure.

It is your time to cross over into fulfillment and to make God's framework the structure that holds up your life. Make this confession today: "I am crossing over!"

Receive God's heavenly strategies. Cross over into your promise. I will see you on the other side!

NOTES

Introduction

1. Dr. Judson Cornwall and Dr. Stelman Smith, *The Exhaustive Dictionary of Bible Names* (North Brunswick, N.J.: Bridge-Logos, 1998), 118.

2. *Webster's American Family Dictionary* (New York: Random House, 1998), "strategy."

3. Ibid.

Chapter 1: The Highway of Holiness

1. Bob Sorge, *Glory When Heaven Invades Earth* (Greenwood, Mich.: Oasis House, 2002), 10.

2. James Strong, *The Enhanced Strong's Lexicon* (Oak Harbor, Wash.: Logos Research Systems, Inc., 1995), #3474.

3. Dr. Wanda Turner, *Celebrate Change* (Shippensburg, Pa.: Treasure House, 2001), 11.

Chapter 2: "Help Me, Lord! I Can't See Where I'm Going!"

1. Cornwall and Smith, *Exhaustive Dictionary*, 47.

2. Ibid., 63.

3. Strong, *Enhanced Strong's Lexicon*, #1763.

4. Ibid., #2119, #5175, #5172.

5. Ibid., #1471, #1342.

6. Ibid., #569.

7. Ibid., #894, #1101.

8. Ibid., #746.

9. Ibid., #495.

10. Ibid., #3448.

11. James Strong, *Strong's Exhaustive Concordance* (Peabody, Mass.: Hendrickson Publishers, 1988), #3068.

12. Ibid., #2451.

13. Strong, *Enhanced Strong's Lexicon*, #1369.

14. Dr. Henry Malone, *Shadow Boxing* (Irving, Tex.: Vision Life Ministries, 1999), 126–127.

Chapter 3: Running with the Horses

1. Strong, *Enhanced Strong's Lexicon*, "redeem."

2. *Webster's*, "time."

3. Spiros Zodhiates, *Hebrew-Greek Key Study Bible* (Nashville, Tenn.: AMG Publishers, 1998), #8474, #2734.

4. Ibid., #6428.

5. I have identified the unclean spirit in my book *Destiny Thieves* (Grand Rapids: Chosen Books, 2007).

Chapter 5: The New Thing

1. Noah Webster, *Noah Webster's First Edition of an American Dictionary of the English Language, 1828* (Chesapeake, Va.: Foundation of American Christian Education, 1967), "structure."

Chapter 6: He Is Back from the Future

1. Strong, *Strong's Exhaustive Concordance*, #8034.

2. Ibid., #760.

3. My book *Destiny Thieves* documents the many ways that the thief steals our destiny and breakthroughs.

Chapter 7: Coming Out of the Wilderness

1. Webster, "wilderness."

2. W. E. Vine, *Vine's Complete Expository of Old and New Testament Words* (Nashville, Tenn.: Thomas Nelson, 1985), "wilderness."

3. Ibid., "tempt."

4. Cornwall and Smith, *Exhaustive Dictionary*, 16.

5. Ibid., 108.

6. Webster, "annoy."

7. Strong, *Enhanced Strong's Lexicon*, #5753, #5771.

8. The "religious spirit" is discussed in detail in my book *Destiny Thieves*.

Chapter 8: Stirring Up Trouble

1. Cornwall and Smith, *Exhaustive Dictionary*, 66.

2. For more information on loss of vision, read *Regaining Vision* by Mickey Freed, available through Zion Ministries: www.zionministries.us or (817) 284-5966.

3. Strong, *Strong's Exhaustive Concordance*, #1080.

Chapter 9: Jumping into the River

1. Cornwall and Smith, *Exhaustive Dictionary*, 204.
2. Ibid., 82.
3. Ibid., 107.
4. Ibid., 74.
5. Ibid., 63.
6. Strong, *Strong's Exhaustive Concordance*, "divination."
7. James Strong, *Strong's Greek and Hebrew Dictionary* (Seattle, Wash.: BibleSoft, 1998), #5592.
8. Barbara Yoder, *The Breaker Anointing* (Ventura, Calif.: Regal Books, 2004), 33–34.
9. Ibid., 34.
10. Ibid., 35.
11. Strong, *Enhanced Strong's Lexicon*, #155.

Chapter 10: Crossing Over into the Promised Land

1. Strong, *Enhanced Strong's Lexicon*, #6030, #6041.
2. Ibid., #5771, #5773.
3. Cornwall and Smith, *Exhaustive Dictionary*, 77.
4. *Webster's*, "cycle."
5. Cornwall and Smith, *Exhaustive Dictionary*, 47.
6. Ibid., 108.
7. Ibid., 16.
8. Ibid., 201.
9. Ibid., 108.
10. *Webster's*, "familiar."
11. Cornwall and Smith, *Exhaustive Dictionary*, 127.
12. Ibid., 124.
13. For more information concerning the –ites in the land, read *The Costly Anointing* by Lori Wilke, published by Destiny Image (1991).
14. Strong, *Enhanced Strong's Lexicon*, #2461, #2459.

Chapter 11: Seekers of His Glory

1. Webster, "occult."
2. Ibid.
3. Ibid.
4. Strong, *Enhanced Strong's Lexicon*, #4363.
5. Ibid., #1390, #1389.
6. Ibid., #1534, #1537, #1556.
7. Ibid., #6428.
8. Ibid., #5783.
9. Ibid., #2336.
10. Ibid., #6873.
11. Ibid., #953.

Chapter 12: Establishing Your Victory Structure

1. Chuck Pierce, *Glory of Zion International Ministries Newsletter*, March 25, 2006.

2. Strong, *Enhanced Strong's Lexicon*, #1919.

Sandie Freed and her husband, Mickey, are the founders and directors of Zion Ministries in Hurst, Texas. Together they pastored a local church in Texas for more than fourteen years, and today they apostolically oversee the Zion Kingdom Training Center.

Sandie is an ordained prophetess with Christian International Ministries and travels extensively teaching prophetic truths to the Body of Christ. Sandie and Mickey also travel nationally and internationally as the Christian International IMPACT Team, in which they apostolically and prophetically oversee regions and churches for their network.

Sandie has written three books, including *Destiny Thieves: Defeat Seducing Spirits and Achieve Your Purpose in God*, and she has been a featured guest on television and radio, where she has shared her testimony of God's healing and delivering power. A gifted minister in dreams and visions and spiritual discernment, Sandie is a sought-after speaker and seminar instructor for her insight on dreams and visions and discerning demonic strongholds over individuals, churches and regions.

Sandie and Mickey have a daughter, Kim, and a son-in-law, Matt, who are active ordained ministers with Zion Ministries.

For more information, contact Sandie at

Zion Ministries
P.O. Box 54874
Hurst, TX 76054
(817) 284-5966 or (817) 589-8811 (office)
email: Zionministries1@sbcglobal.net
website: www.zionministries.us